Dr Robert Baldwin, is married to Sharon. They have three children and four grandchildren. Born in Powys, Mid Wales, he studied medicine at the Welsh National School of Medicine, Cardiff, from where he graduated in 1977. Aged 18, he became a Christian believer, and alongside his medical career, followed a calling to be a Christian pastor. He has worked as both a general medical practitioner and as a Christian pastor, in South Wales and Bristol, England.

This book is dedicated to my wife, Sharon, who has been a constant support and help to me, as I have pursued the two vocations of doctor and pastor.

Robert Baldwin

BE HEALED, BE WHOLE

Discover your healing

AUSTIN MACAULEY PUBLISHERS™
LONDON · CAMBRIDGE · NEW YORK · SHARJAH

Copyright © Robert Baldwin 2024

The right of Robert Baldwin to be identified as the author of this work has been asserted by the author in accordance with Sections 77 and 78 of the Copyright, Designs and Patents Act 1988.

All rights reserved. No part of this publication may be reproduced, stored in a retrieval system, or transmitted in any form or by any means, electronic, mechanical, photocopying, recording, or otherwise, without the prior permission of the publishers.

Any person who commits any unauthorised act in relation to this publication may be liable to criminal prosecution and civil claims for damages.

The story, experiences, and words are the author's alone.

A CIP catalogue record for this title is available from the British Library.

ISBN 9781035851478 (Paperback)
ISBN 9781035851485 (ePub e-book)

www.austinmacauley.com

First Published 2024
Austin Macauley Publishers Ltd®
1 Canada Square
Canary Wharf
London
E14 5AA

The many patients that I have treated, the congregations that I have had the privilege of leading, and all the Christian leaders, who have inspired me, challenged me, and taught me so much.

My wife and family, for always being there for me and being a constant source of encouragement.

Austin Macauley Publishers for assisting me in getting this book to publication.

To them all, I say, "A big thank you - Diolch yn fawr!"

Introduction

As a Christian believer, a pastor, and a doctor, I have always been fascinated by the subject of Divine healing. In the late 1980s, I wrote a book, entitled *Healing and Wholeness*. Since then, not only have I experienced God's healing touch in my own life but have evidenced it in the lives of many others, and therefore felt it was the right time to write another book on healing.

In this book, I have incorporated some of those experiences and also attempted to update or enlarge upon some of the things included in the first book. I have sought to give a balanced, uncomplicated view to the subject of healing, whilst at the same time, hopefully, helping those who are seeking healing, discover their healing. For those who have been prayed for many times, but still have not experienced healing (yet), then hopefully, you too, in the pages of this book, will find encouragement.

For those who want to start praying for and ministering to the sick, I have included chapters on how we can all be used, by the Holy Spirit, in this wonderful ministry. All the healing stories, in this book, are true stories. Occasionally, I have used fictitious names to safeguard the identity of the individual concerned.

When all is said and done, the most important healing of all is for a person to accept Jesus Christ as their Lord and Saviour. The worst thing that could happen to a person is to have healing of their body and then neglect their soul. God is a healing God and He loves to touch and heal people, but most of all, He loves for people to come into relationship with Him, through His Son, Jesus. One of the most well-known verses of the Bible is:

> For God so loved the world that He gave His only begotten Son, that whoever believes in Him should not perish but have everlasting life. (John 3:16)[1].

If you are not a Christian, then begin your healing journey by accepting Jesus as your Saviour. He is the spotless, pure Son of God, who became flesh and willingly died on the cross, in our place, to take the punishment of all our sin and wrongdoing—that separates us from God. Three days later, He rose from the dead. The resurrection demonstrates that His sacrifice has been accepted, our sins can be forgiven, and we can have eternal life. Not only that, but we can become children of God and part of God's great family. He is only a prayer away—invite Him into your life today!

Be blessed and encouraged as you read.

Rob Baldwin

---

[1] All Bible references in this book, unless otherwise stated, are from the New King James Version.

Chapter 1
The Big C

The pain was excruciating. I felt faint and clammy.

I was in the middle of an evening surgery when, suddenly, out of nowhere, the pain in my left side started. I informed the receptionist that I was unwell. She sent in the only other clinician left in the building—a midwife!

Great, I thought, *In a moment, she is going to say, 'Push'*. I knew and she knew that I was experiencing renal colic. Severe pain in the kidney caused by a trapped stone. After an hour, the pain subsided. I made my way to the out-of-hours emergency GP service.

There, the duty doctor agreed that it was likely I had been experiencing renal colic. He gave me medication to control any further pain and recommended that I see my own general practitioner.

My own GP was in touch the next day. She said that the gold standard investigation for renal colic was a CT scan, looking at the kidneys, ureters and bladder. I agreed, and this was arranged by the GP. Within a week the appointment came through. I had the CT scan and thought nothing more of it—until the next day, when I had a telephone call asking me to go back for a further CT scan, which would include my chest and abdomen. *This is more than a kidney stone*, I thought.

The repeat scan, including my chest, was done. The attending radiographer asked if I would like to see the consultant radiologist who was present in the building. I said, "Yes, please."

I was ushered into his office and sat down, looking at the screen set in front of myself and the radiologist. I felt like I was back at medical school, as he went ahead and explained what I was seeing on the screen. First, he showed me a sizeable kidney stone. This had undoubtedly caused my earlier pain.

He then said, "And there is this." He pointed out a 7 cm diameter mass extending from the upper pole of my left kidney. He went on to say, "In my view, this has all the appearances of a renal cell carcinoma. That is the unwelcome news. The good news is that I can see no spread to the rest of your abdomen or chest."

For a moment, I thought I was looking at the scan of another patient, and then it hit me—"It's me!"

I was overcome with emotion as I tried to explain what had just happened, to my wife, who had been sitting in an adjoining waiting room. Even after phoning our children, I still could not believe this was happening. In my mid-fifties, I had cancer. That night, I could not sleep. My mind was working overtime!

I thought to myself, *Okay, I am a Christian believer. I know that I know if I die, I will go to heaven. My faith is firmly in Jesus who died and rose again and because He lives, I live.*

My mind went over all the things that I had shared with many others in the same situation. However, that did not stop me from thinking about my wife and children and how they would cope. It was a restless start to the night! I then determined to do something to change that. "I will pray through the Names of God." I cannot recollect having done that before, but I began to go through the Jehovah compound Names of God, as found in the Old Testament.

The first name was Jehovah-Tsidkenu—God my righteousness. I spent time thanking God for what Jesus did for me on the cross. He, who knew no sin, became sin for me that I might be made the righteousness of God in Him. I asked God to search my heart and cleanse me of all sin. I thanked Him for the power of His blood.

I then went onto Jehovah-Mekaddeshem—the Lord who sanctifies. I thanked God that he had set me apart for Himself that I was not only his child, but that he had called me into Christian ministry. I thanked God for the work that He had done through me, but also prayed about what He would still do through me and rededicated my life to Him.

I then came to Jehovah-Rapha—God who heals. I prayed, "Lord, you are the Healer. I believe in Divine healing, and no matter what doctors may say, I believe you can heal me." I expected to feel a Divine hand come and touch me and everything would be all right. That did not happen—at least not in the way I expected. I moved on to pray Jehovah-Nissi—God my banner/my protector.

At the time I did not understand why, but I began to feel a sense of peace when I prayed this Name of God. I prayed to Jehovah-Jireh—God who provides. I thanked God that no matter what happened, He would provide. I moved on to Jehovah-Rohi—God my shepherd. I thanked God that whatever I was going to go through, He would be there with me.

I recited to myself Psalm 23. I then prayed Jehovah-Shalom—God my peace. I thanked God for His peace that passes all understanding.

Praying through the Names of God, focussed my mind for some time. However, I was still not sleeping. I decided to pray through the Names of God once more. I got as far as Jehovah-Nissi—the Lord my protector. As I thanked God for His protection, a deep peace hit me, and I fell fast asleep!

Over the next months, I was going to prove, over and over again, that God truly was my protector. Already, I could see that the kidney stone, as painful as it had been, had alerted the doctors to what was going on in my body. Protection. In a matter of weeks, I was scheduled for a left nephrectomy.

On the day of the surgery, I said to the surgeon, "I believe in the power of prayer. Can you please check before removing the kidney, whether the tumour is still there." The operation went ahead, and the left kidney was removed. Not what I was hoping for, but the surgeon was confident that there had been no spread of the tumour and that it was localised within the left kidney.

A week after the surgery, the wound became very reddened, and the area around the wound was swollen. I was not eating and felt terrible. The wound was infected. Back into the hospital I went. A litre of pus was drained from the wound.

The wound was packed, and I was in hospital for some days. During that stay, the consultant came to see me. He said, "With a laparoscopic nephrectomy, I normally sew up the abdominal wall and skin with one piece of suture material. However, when I did your nephrectomy, I had a Greek doctor helping me who said that where he came from, they sewed up the abdomen in layers, even in a laparoscopic procedure. So that is what we did. Just as well, because if we had not, the infection would have tracked down into your abdomen and that would have been extremely serious."

I thought, *Thank you, Lord. You truly are Jehovah-Nissi.*

A week after I was discharged from the hospital, my own GP phoned me. She told me that one of the scans that had been done, when I had been readmitted with the infection, showed a lesion on my descending/sigmoid colon. She recommended that I go for a sigmoidoscopy. A month or so later, I had a sigmoidoscopy. The endoscopist discovered a large polyp on my sigmoid colon. The histology report showed that this was a precancerous polyp. Again, I thought, *Thank you, Lord. You are the amazing Jehovah-Nissi.*

It is now over 14 years since I had the surgery. Every year, I have a scan and chest X-ray, and every year, the result comes back the same. "All clear from any signs of cancer." Every year, I thank God that He is truly Jehovah-Nissi although I hasten to add that I now, not just annually, but every day, pray through the Names of God, as part of my daily prayer routine.

I not only reflect on what each name means, but I then use that name to pray not only for myself but others. For example, when praying the name Jehovah-Nissi, I begin by praying for protection for my family, then I move on to pray for all the different church leaders that I am in close relationship with, for my neighbours, for the nation—particularly the prime minister and the cabinet and then onto the nations and Christians facing tough times in those nations—such as persecution. On different days, I will major in one name more than the others. To the list of the seven Jehovah compound names, I have added Jehovah-Shammah—the God who is there. Whatever we go through, He is there with us.

Praying through the Names of God is extremely powerful. Jesus said, repeatedly, "Whatever you ask in My Name, that I will do, that the Father may be glorified in the Son. If you ask anything in My Name, I will do it" (John 14:13-14, John 15:16, John 16:23-24).

If you cannot remember all the Names of God, then do not worry, they are all added together in the name of Jesus. Jesus is our righteousness (2 Corinthians 5:21), Jesus is our sanctifier (Hebrews 13:12, Ephesians 5:26), Jesus is our Healer (Isaiah 53:5, 1 Peter 2:24), Jesus is our protector (Mark 16:17-18), Jesus is our provider (Philippians 4:19), Jesus is our shepherd (John 10;11,14) and Jesus is our peace (John 14:27).

Another way of praying through the Names of God is to pray through Psalm 23. The Lord is my shepherd (J. Rohi); I shall not want (J. Jireh). He makes me lie down in green pastures: He leads me beside the still waters (J. Shalom). He restores my soul (J. Rapha); He leads me in the paths of righteousness for His name's sake (J. Tsidkenu).

Yea, though I walk through the valley of the shadow of death, I will fear no evil; for You are with me; Your rod and Your staff comfort me (J. Shammah). You prepare a table before me in the presence of my enemies (J. Nissi); You anoint my head with oil; my cup runs over (J. Mekeddeshem). Then end the prayer thanking God for His grace (undeserved mercy and love)—surely goodness and mercy shall follow me all the days of my life and thanking Him for the assurance of your eternal dwelling place—and I will dwell in the house of the Lord forever. Psalm 23 and the Names of God are both, what I call, pattern prayers. Prayers that we can use to build our own prayers.

A pattern prayer that Jesus gave is the prayer that we call the Lord's Prayer. I do not believe that the Lord intended us to just recite that prayer in a matter of seconds, but rather to use it as a structure on which to build our own prayers. In fact, He introduces the prayer by saying:

> In this manner, therefore pray. (Matthew 6:9)

The words, in this manner, can also be translated, after this pattern. Used in this way, the Lord's prayer can be broken down into seven sections. If we spend ten minutes, praying and meditating in each section, we will have prayed over one hour! For example, when you get to the phrase, "Hallowed be Your Name," then we can go through the Names of God. We can take our time on each one, reflecting on what each one means and then praying it into our situation.

Chris Hodges, Senior Pastor of Church of the Highlands, and a New York Times Bestselling author, has written an excellent book which covers various patterns that we can use in prayer. The book is called, *Pray First: The Transformative Power of a Life Built on Prayer*.[2]

---

[2] Chris Hodges (2023), *Pray First*, Nelson Books.

Chapter 2
The God Who Heals

It was a Thursday night, and I was the on-call junior doctor for general surgery. I was told that a man was on his way in with intestinal obstruction. Sure enough, when he arrived, he was vomiting; he was in pain; and his abdomen was distended. Because he was so unwell, he was admitted to a side cubicle. As I arrived to see him, a nurse was completing her admission questionnaire.

At the same moment when I was coming through the doorway, she was asking, "And what is your religion, sir?" He replied, "I'm a Christian. I belong to the Elim Pentecostal Church." As he said those words, in a moment of time, the Holy Spirit took me to the book of Exodus, in the Old Testament, chapter fifteen, where it says:

> I will put none of the diseases on you which I have brought on the Egyptians. For I am the Lord who heals you.
> Then they came to Elim, where there were twelve wells of water and seventy palm trees; so, they camped there by the waters. (Exodus 15:26-27)

After introducing myself and saying how delighted I was that he went to an Elim Church, I shared these Scriptures with the man. At that moment I longed to pray with him, but also knew that I had a job to do. I took his history (of the complaint), asked the usual additional medical questions, such as his medication history, and then went ahead to examine him. It was not difficult to make a diagnosis. He was, indeed, suffering from some form of intestinal obstruction.

A range of blood tests and an abdominal X-ray were ordered. I then said to the patient, "I'm a Christian as well. I believe in the power of prayer. Would it be okay for me to pray for you?" He agreed to be prayed for. I felt a powerful sense of the Holy Spirit upon me, as I prayed for him. I recited the Scripture verse that I had quoted earlier, about God being the Lord who heals us, declaring it over him, as I prayed.

Given the severity of the man's symptoms, it was likely that he was going to be in hospital for some time and highly likely that he would require emergency surgery to deal with the cause of the obstruction. However, after prayer, the symptoms began to ease. He was kept in for the next three days, for observation. When I next saw him, it was early on the following Monday morning. Before starting work on the ward that I was assigned to, I decided to go and look at this man.

As I walked down the corridor, lo and behold, the man was walking in the opposite direction with a small suitcase in his hand. I said, "Are you off home then."

He replied, "Yes. After your prayer, the symptoms disappeared, and I've been symptom-free the past two days. This morning the ward discharged me!" The joy that I felt at that moment knew no limits. Jehovah-Rapha, the God who heals, had touched this man!

God heals: healing within us

God's name, Jehovah-Rapha, means 'I am the Lord who heals you'. Fantastic. But how does that work? I want to introduce you to several ways that God heals. Firstly, there is healing within us. When God created Adam and Eve, Genesis 1 verse 26-27 says:

> Then God said, "Let Us make man in Our image, according to Our likeness... So, God created man in His own image; in the image of God, He created him; male and female He created them."

The phrase created in the image of God could mean several things. For example, God is a three-part being (Father, Son, Holy Spirit) yet one. We too are a three-part being—spirit, soul, and body (1 Thessalonians 5:23), yet one. We will look at this more closely, later in the book. Created in the image of God could also mean that we are created superior and different to animals.

These qualities include morality, reason, creativity, generosity, and self-worth. Yes, these qualities have been messed up through the fall of man, but nonetheless, they are still traceable in every human being. To that list we can add, to be created in the image of Jehovah-Rapha is to be created with healing within us. God has made us with an amazing immune and body repair system.

As children, most of us would have encountered the chicken pox virus. An irritating spotty rash that blisters, scabs, and then fades away. True, the virus may linger in the posterior root ganglion of our nervous system and cause shingles in later life, but as far as having chicken pox again, in a healthy individual, the immune system now recognises the chicken pox virus and is ready to fight it, should we encounter it again.

The same could be said for other viruses—provided they do not change! The same is true for vaccinations. For example, at around fifteen months old, a child receives a vaccination against measles. Through vaccination, the immune system is primed to recognise the measles virus and protect the child from an illness that can be potentially serious.

Then, there is our body repair system. If we wound ourselves or break a bone, the body has a repair system to cause clotting of bleeding vessels and then start the process of healing and knitting wounds and fractured bones (provided they are not displaced). Okay, this is putting it all very simply, but if you were to study these processes in detail, you would be amazed at the healing system God has placed within us.

When a surgeon removes damaged or diseased tissue, or resets broken bones, then that surgeon relies upon the healing system, made by God, to complete the healing and repair. So, when someone is about to have surgery, it is fine to pray that God will not only guide the hands of the surgeon but grant that person a speedy recovery. We can pray that God will quicken the healing and repair system He has created us with. When they have made a full recovery, we can give thanks to God, who provided us with healing within us.

Healing in nature

When God created Adam and Eve, He created them to have communion with Him. Genesis chapter three tells us that God would come and commune with them in the cool of the day. It must have been a wonderful thing to have such close fellowship with God. However, when God created humankind, He did not make robots who would slavishly do His bidding, but He created us with free will. We can choose whether we want to fellowship with God or not.

When you consider the love and blessings that God wants to pour out on us, then it is a no-brainer to not want to spend time with Him! However, through the deception of Satan (the serpent), Adam and Eve made a choice to do something that God told them not to do. God had said:

> Of every tree of the garden you may freely eat; but the tree of the knowledge of good and evil you shall not eat, for in the day you eat of it you shall surely die. (Genesis 2:17)

Satan, previously known as Lucifer—a magnificent archangel who became proud and wanted to be equal with God and, as a result of this, was thrown out of heaven—knew better than anyone that God is a just God. If God punished him for pride and disobedience, then God would have to do the same with Adam and Eve. As you read Genesis chapter three you can almost hear Satan, the serpent's, beguiling words, "Has God said…? You will not surely die. You will be like God, knowing good and evil."

With Adam standing by (why didn't he stop her?), Eve gets taken in by Satan's deceptive narrative and eats the forbidden fruit. She then hands it to Adam, who eats it as well. Tragedy. It suddenly dawns on them what they have just done. They feel exposed to their nakedness and immediately try to 'cover up' using fig leaves.

God is the all-knowing God, and I love how that when He comes calling for them, rather than pointing an accusing finger, He gets them to confess what they have done.

> Then the Lord God called to Adam and said to him, "Where are you?" So, he said, "I heard your voice in the garden, and I was afraid because I was naked; and I hid myself." And He said, "Who told you that you were naked? Have you eaten from the tree of which I commanded that you should not eat?" (Genesis 3:9-11).

God is just, and it must have been with a broken heart that God metes out punishment upon the serpent and upon Adam and Eve for their sinful action. An act of disobedience, brought about by listening to the narrative of Satan the serpent, sees not only a perfect world disrupted but leads to the onset of sickness, suffering and death. However, amid the sentence of punishment, we catch glimpses of the loving heart of God. In His words of punishment to Satan, God says:

> "And I will put enmity between you and the woman, and between your seed and her Seed: He shall bruise your head, and you shall bruise His heel." (Genesis 3:15)

This is a messianic prophecy, telling us that from the seed of the woman, the Saviour will be born. Satan may 'bruise His heel' refers to the cross, but the Saviour 'bruises Satan's head' refers to the ultimate victory of the cross. All is not lost; God has a plan of redemption! Another glimpse of the loving heart of God is found in God's words to Adam:

> "Cursed is the ground for your sake; in toil you shall eat of it all the days of your life. Both thorns and thistles it shall bring forth to you, and you shall eat the herb of the field." (Genesis 3:17-18)

Amid a punishment for wilful disobedience, not only do we find the future promise of a Saviour, but we also find a means to ease the pain and suffering that ensued.

"You shall eat *the herb of the field.*"

In amongst the herbs of the field, mankind would find herbs to ease pain and suffering. One of the most powerful painkillers known to man, used routinely in such situations as post-operative pain and pain relief in terminally ill patients, is diamorphine. Diamorphine, also known as heroine, is derived from the opium poppy[3]—literally the herb of the field. Another well-known painkiller is aspirin. Aspirin (a salicylate) is found in many plants, including the bark of the willow tree[4] (I am not suggesting that next time you have a headache, you go and chew on the nearest willow tree!).

---

[3] Encyclopaedia Britannica. Opium poppy/Description, Drugs and Seeds.

[4] Bartram's 1998 Encyclopaedia of Herbal Medicine. History of willow in medicine.

Beyond pain relief, we find relief for many other conditions, in *the herbs of the field*. When I first started practising medicine, a drug that was in common use for heart conditions such as heart failure and atrial fibrillation, was digoxin. In its herbal form, it is digitalis, extracted from the fox glove flower[5]. Then there is ephedrine from the stem and branches of the Ephedra sinica plant[6]. This is a stimulant drug, not used nowadays, but in the past was used to help with breathing in conditions such as asthma.

Then take penicillin. Discovered by Alexander Fleming in 1928[7], Fleming noticed that a mould growing on a petri dish of the bacteria staphylococcus, stopped the bacteria from growing when it met the bacteria. Just a few examples of healing within nature. A Biblical example of the use of herbs in healing is found in 2 Kings chapter 20. Hezekiah, the king, has become sick, and it looks as though he may die.

In fact, Isaiah, the prophet, goes to him and tells him that he is going to die! Hezekiah cries out to the Lord in prayer. God tells Isaiah the prophet to go back to Hezekiah and tell him that God had heard his prayer and will heal him. The story continues:

> Then Isaiah said, "Take a lump of figs." So, they took and laid it on the boil, and he (Hezekiah) recovered. (2 Kings 20:7)

---

[5] MedlinePlus Medical Encyclopaedia. Digitalis.
[6] ScienceDirect. Ephedra sinica—an overview.
[7] American Chemical Society. Alexander Fleming's Discovery and Development of Penicillin.

What the exact ingredient was that killed the infection or if it was just a physical action used to administer the healing power of God, we are not told. The point, I am trying to make, is that God has placed within nature the means to alleviate human sickness and suffering.

The prophet Ezekiel, in chapter forty-seven of his prophecy, has a vision of a river, the source of which is the very temple of God. Along the side of that river, he sees trees and he makes this observation:

> Their fruit will be for food, and their leaves for medicine. (Ezekiel 47:12)

In the last chapter of the Bible, the Apostle John also has a vision of a river, and he writes:

> In the middle of the street, and on either side of the river, was the tree of life, which bore twelve fruits, each tree yielding its fruit every month. The leaves of the tree were for the healing of the nations. (Revelation 22:2)

This may well be figurative, prophetic language, but it does, once again, convey the thought of medicinal properties in certain plants.

Most of the drugs used in modern medicine find their origins in natural ingredients such as herbs. The modern pharmaceutical industry has developed them into newer and more efficient (herbalists may disagree!) products. The author and originator of it all is God. So, when a doctor prescribes a medication that alleviates our suffering and controls a condition that could cause us injury, then we can say, "Thank you, Lord. You have provided the means to ease my pain and suffering." Healing within nature.

Healing within the Law

In Exodus chapter 15 verse 26, God said, "If you diligently heed the voice of the Lord your God and do what is right in His sight, give ear to His commandments and keep all His statutes, I will put none of the diseases on you which I have brought on the Egyptians. For I am the Lord who heals you." It should not surprise us then, to find healing within the law. Here is a sample. For starters, there are a host of dietary laws.

Foods that can be eaten and foods that cannot be eaten (Leviticus 18). Then there are laws about quarantine of infectious diseases such as leprosy and bodily discharges (Leviticus 13-15). Laws about sanitation (Deuteronomy 23:12-13). Laws about washing (Exodus 30:17-20). Laws about sexual morality (Leviticus 18).

In the recent COVID-19 pandemic, before vaccines became available, the mainstay of prevention was hand washing and quarantine. The words, 'Hands, face, space', could have been extracted from the book of Leviticus! Eating properly prepared food, having clean drinking water and good sanitation, remain essentials for any group of people.

To all the above, we can add adequate rest. God instructed His people to have one day, the Sabbath Day, when they rested from all their work. This was one of the ten commandments (Exodus 20:8-11). God Himself, set the example. In six days, He created the heavens and the earth and on the seventh day, He rested.

Add to that regular rest day, several other holy days (holidays). For example, at the Feast of Tabernacles, the Jewish people were instructed to camp out in temporary shelters for seven days. What fun that would have been!

How much stress-induced illness would be avoided if people had a regular rest day and regular restful holidays? In fact, the first man Adam, after God created him, rested on his first day. In other words, Adam worked from rest. How good is that! We tend to work and then rest. It may seem like a play on words, but there is something extremely healthy about working from a place of rest.

We could add to these Old Testament Laws, the New Testament concept that our bodies are the temple of the Holy Spirit. It is important that we keep our bodies/our temples in as tip-top condition as we can, through exercise and a balanced diet, coupled with appropriate rest, and that we avoid harmful substances such as excess alcohol and smoking.

So we have healing within us, healing within nature and healing within the law. As we turn the pages of the Bible to the New Testament, we discover that healing goes up to another gear altogether.

Chapter 3
New Testament Healing

He was dressed in camel skin with a leather belt around his waist. His face was deeply tanned from long hours in the desert sun and his diet was a little unusual, consisting of locusts and wild honey. His message was straight and to the point, "Repent for the kingdom of God (literally the rule of God) is at hand." His name is John the Baptist, the forerunner of Jesus.

John proclaimed his message somewhere in the southern part of the Jordan River. Recognising from Old Testament prophecies (Isaiah 40:1-5, Malachi 3:1) that this could be the forerunner of the promised Messiah, crowds quickly gathered, to hear the preaching of John and submit to John's baptism—a symbolic washing away of sin.

One day, Jesus Himself shows up. John points to him and says, "Behold! The Lamb of God who takes away the sin of the world!" (John 1:29). Jesus submits to John's baptism, but whilst the rest of the people confessed their sins, Jesus, the spotless, pure Son of God, comes straight up out of the water. The heavens open and as the Spirit of God descends on Jesus, in the form of a dove, God the Father speaks and says, "This is My beloved Son in whom I am ell pleased" (Matthew 3:17).

Following a time of fasting in the wilderness with Satan trying to tempt Jesus (and miserably failing!), Jesus is ready to commence his ministry. The Gospel writer, Luke, points out the importance of the Holy Spirit.

> And the Holy Spirit descended in bodily form like a dove upon Him. (Luke 3:22)
> Then Jesus, being filled with the Holy Spirit, returned from the Jordan, and was led by the Spirit into the wilderness. (Luke 4:1)
> Then Jesus returned in the power of the Spirit to Galilee. (Like 4:14)
> The Spirit of the Lord is upon Me. (Luke 4:18)

Jesus is 100% God and 100% man, in one person, Jesus Christ, the anointed one. That said, Luke shows that Jesus chose not to perform His ministry in the power of the God nature within Him but in the power of the God nature that came upon Him. That is the person of the Holy Spirit. As we shall discover in later chapters, if we are going to be used to bring healing, in the same way that Jesus did, it is going to be in the power and anointing of the Holy Spirit.

So, following His wilderness experience, Jesus begins His ministry. Matthew records:

> From that time Jesus began to preach and to say, "Repent for the kingdom of heaven (synonymous to kingdom of God, as used in the other Gospels) is at hand." (Matthew 4:17)

The phrase 'kingdom of heaven (or God) is at hand' could be amplified as "the liberating rule of God, which liberates from sin and sickness and reveals a new way of living, is within your grasp." This was certainly good news for the people, as Matthew goes on to explain.

> And Jesus went about all Galilee, preaching the Gospel of the kingdom, and healing all kinds of sickness and all kinds of disease among the people. Then His fame went throughout all Syria, and they brought to Him all sick people who were afflicted with various diseases and torments, and those who were demon-possessed, epileptics and paralytics and He healed them. (Matthew 4:23-24)

As you read the four Gospels, then story after story unfolds of individuals and whole groups healed by Jesus. The blind see, the deaf hear, the dumb speak, the lame walk and lepers are cleansed. The word Gospel means good news, and that was certainly good news!

You might be thinking, "That was then, but what about now?" Here is the 'good news', what Jesus did during His three years of ministry upon earth, has now been made available to us through the finished work of the cross and the ministry of the Holy Spirit.

The Cross

Isaiah the prophet prophesied some six to seven hundred years before Christ. In Isaiah chapter 53, we have what is the greatest single Old Testament chapter prophesying of the atoning work that would be accomplished by Jesus. As you read this amazing chapter, you cannot help but notice that alongside the forgiveness of sins is the clear mention of the healing of sickness.

> Surely, He has borne our griefs (pain) and carried our sorrows (sickness); yet we esteemed Him stricken, smitten by God, and afflicted. But He was wounded for our transgressions, He was bruised for our iniquities; the chastisement for our peace was upon Him, and by His stripes we are healed. (Isaiah 53:4-5)

Matthew, the Gospel writer, quotes from Isaiah when writing about Jesus's healing ministry.

> When evening had come, they brought to Him many who were demon-possessed, and He cast out the spirits with a word, and healed all who were sick, that it might be fulfilled which was spoken by Isaiah the prophet, saying: "He Himself took our infirmities and bore our sicknesses." (Matthew 8:16-17)

The Apostle Peter, in his first epistle, ties the Isaiah fifty-three text directly to the finished work of the cross.

> Who himself bore our sins in His own body on the tree, that we, having died to sins, might live for righteousness—by whose stripes you were healed. (1 Peter 2:24)

The cross was not an accident. It was the very plan of God to save mankind. Preachers in the past loved to use the same letter or similar-sounding words to make points in their sermons. For the message of the cross, we could use the letter 'V'. The sacrifice of Jesus on the cross was:

> Virtuous—He was (and is) the spotless, pure Son of God. (1 Peter 1:19)
> Voluntary—Jesus went freely to the cross. In Gethsemane, He prayed to the Father, "Not my will, but your will be done." (Matthew 26:39)
> Vicarious—He took our place. He who knew no sin became sin for us. (2 Corinthians 5:21)
> Victorious—He cried out, "It is finished!" (John 19:30). Once, for all. (Hebrews 9:12, 28, 10:10, 12)

But remember, it was not just for sins but for sickness too. The forgiveness of sins and the healing of sickness go together, like hand in glove. We read in Psalm one hundred and three.

> Bless the Lord, O my soul, and forget not all His benefits: who forgives all your iniquities, who heals all your diseases. (Psalm 103:2-3)

We have already quoted from Isaiah fifty-three, where, in verse five, the prophet says, "He was wounded for our transgressions, He was bruised for our iniquities... and by His stripes we are healed."

In the New Testament, on one occasion, Jesus is in a house. The place is packed out and Luke says, "The power of the Lord was present to heal them" (Luke 5:17). A paralysed man is brought by four friends, who, on finding they cannot get in because of the crowds, climb up on the roof (possibly a thin roof shade over a courtyard), make a hole, and lower their friend at the feet of Jesus. Luke continues:

> When He (Jesus) saw their faith, He said to him, "Man your sins are forgiven you." And the scribes and Pharisees began to reason, saying, "Who is this who speaks blasphemies? Who can forgive sins but God alone?"
> But when Jesus perceived their thoughts, He answered and said to them, "Why are you reasoning in your hearts? Which is easier to say, 'Your sins be forgiven you', or to say, rise and walk?"
> "But that you may know that the Son of Man has power on earth to forgive sins (Jesus is making a direct statement about His deity)"—He said to the man who was paralysed, "I say to you, arise, take up your bed, and go to your house."
> Immediately he rose up before them, took up what he had been lying on, and departed to his own house, glorifying God. (Luke 5:20:25)

Forgiveness of sins and healing of sickness—Jesus does both! You might be thinking, "Yes, that was then, but what about now?" Through the finished work of the cross, the power of the resurrection:

> But to you who fear My Name, the Sun of Righteousness shall arise with healing in His wings (light beams). (Malachi 4:2)

And with the coming of the Holy Spirit, both forgiveness of sins and healing of sickness have been made available to us. How do we receive it? The simple answer is 'By faith'. You might say, "But I don't have faith." That's fine; in the next chapter, we explore where faith comes from—and it is certainly not a blind, wishful-thinking type of faith!

Chapter 4
Faith

In over forty-five years of ministry, one of the saddest things I have encountered is when people have said, "The preacher said that I am not healed because I don't have faith." Such comments make the sick person feel that they are a weak, second-class Christian. It has been liberating for those people to hear the words, "It is not your faith. God gives us faith." The writer of Hebrews tells us that Jesus is the author and finisher of faith (Hebrews 12:2).

In his letter to the Ephesians, Paul, in writing about salvation, is very clear about this.

> For by grace, you have been saved through faith, and that not of yourselves; it is the gift of God, not of works, lest anyone should boast. (Ephesians 2:8)

Does that apply to sickness? Well, we have already seen a clear link between the forgiveness of sins and the healing of sickness. Look at Acts chapter three. In this chapter, we have the well-known story of the healing of the lame man who was sat begging at the gate of the temple called Beautiful. Peter and John (recently filled with the Holy Spirit and commissioned by Jesus) are on their way up to the temple, at the hour of prayer.

The man, as was his custom, over many years, was sat there begging. This was likely to have been his only source of income. The Bible tells us that he had been born with a deformity of his feet and ankles (possible club feet). As Peter and John pass him, he manages to get their attention. The Scripture records the following:

> And fixing his eyes on him, with John, Peter said, "Look at us." So, he gave them his full attention, expecting to receive something from them. Peter said, "Silver and gold I do not have, but what I do have I give you: In the name of Jesus Christ of Nazareth, rise up and walk."
> And he took him by the right hand and lifted him up, and immediately his feet and ankle bones received strength. So, he, leaping up, stood, and walked and entered the temple with them—walking and leaping and praising God. And all the people saw him walking, leaping, and praising God. (Acts 3:4-9)

What an amazing miracle! To say it caused a stir would be an understatement. A previously crippled man, who everyone, who attended the temple, knew, walking and leaping and praising God. The fact he can go into the temple is further confirmation of the healing miracle, as sick and crippled people were not allowed to enter. Soon the crowds gather, and Peter addresses them sharing the message of the cross and explaining how the miracle occurred. With regard to the miracle, Peter says this:

> And His name (Jesus), through faith in His name, has made this man strong, whom you see and know. Yes, the faith which comes through Him has given him this perfect soundness in the presence of you all. (Acts 3:16)

Note the phrase, 'the faith which comes'. The lame man had no faith. He was begging and concentrating on eking out a living, but as Peter, with Holy Spirit authority, spoke the name of Jesus, something happened——faith came. And in response to that faith, a miracle occurred.

Faith can come in one of three ways. Faith can come by the word, by the Name or by the Holy Spirit.

Faith comes by the word

Two Greek words are used in the New Testament to describe 'the word of God'. One is 'logos'. This refers more to the general word of God. The other is 'rama'. This refers to the specific word of God for any given situation or time. In Romans chapter ten, the Apostle Paul writes:

> So, then faith comes by hearing and hearing by the word of God. (Romans 10:17)

The word 'rama' is used here.[8] It is also used in Matthew chapter four:

---

[8] Young's Analytical Concordance to the Bible.

> Man shall not live by bread alone, but by every word that proceeds (and keeps on proceeding) from the mouth of God. (Matthew 4:4)

We can be reading the Bible—the general word of God, and suddenly a Scripture comes alive and speaks to us—the specific, 'rama' word, to us at that moment in time. The same can happen when listening to a preacher. They are preaching a general message but then a word comes alive to us and speaks to us, personally. This is how faith comes by the word. Paul writes of this in Romans chapter 10:

> How shall they call on Him in whom they have not believed? And how shall they believe in Him of whom they have not heard? And how shall they hear without a preacher? (Romans 10:14)

Hebrews chapter eleven gives us a list of great men and women of faith. One of them was Abraham. Abram (as he was originally called) lived in the Ur of the Chaldees. It is likely that he was a moon worshipper. At that point in his life, he did not have faith. But then God spoke to him:

> Get out of your country, from your family and from your father's house to a land that I will show you. I will make you a great nation; I will bless you and make your name great; and you shall be a blessing. I will bless those who bless you, and curse those who curses you; and in you all the families of the earth will be blessed. (Genesis 12:1-3)

Faith came by the word of God! Abraham left the Ur of the Chaldees not on a whim but on a word. He knew that he knew that God had spoken. Even though, at that point, he did not know his destination, faith burned in his heart. As Hebrews chapter eleven verse one says:

> Now faith is the substance of things hoped for, the evidence of things not seen.

It is substance—we know that we know deep in our hearts it is real, and the evidence is, God has said it, so although we can't see it, we know it is going to happen! That is how it was for Abraham.

Take Joshua. He faced a daunting task following in the footsteps of Moses, that is, until God spoke to him.

> It came to pass that the Lord spoke to Joshua the son of Nun, Moses' assistant, saying, "Moses My servant is dead. Now therefore, arise, go over this Jordan, you and all this people, to the land which I am giving to them—the children of Israel. Every place that the sole of your foot will tread upon I have given you, as I said to Moses…" (Joshua 1:1-3)

With that word came the faith for the task that lay ahead. We could cite many more examples of people who received a word from God. A word that created faith and enabled them to do great exploits for God. Hebrews chapter 11 gives a whole list.

In the New Testament, a centurion whose servant is sick comes to Jesus. This man, who by virtue of his rank, had been given authority (by Caesar) to lead and give orders to soldiers, perceived a similar authority in Jesus. He recognised that Jesus was submitted to God's authority, and because of that, He spoke with authority. When he comes to Jesus on behalf of his sick servant, he says:

> "Lord my servant is lying at home paralysed, dreadfully tormented." And Jesus said to him, "I will come and heal him." The centurion answered and said, "Lord, I am not worthy that You should come under my roof. But only speak a word, and my servant will be healed. For I am also a man under authority, having soldiers under me. And I say to this one, 'Go', and he goes; and to another 'Come', and he comes; and to my servant, 'Do this', and he does it." (Matthew 8:6-8)

Note how the centurion had grasped the importance of 'a word' spoken with authority, releases a healing miracle.

When I was forty years old, one morning I was woken by the sound of my own heartbeat. What was particularly alarming was that it was irregular. Every third beat was missing. That morning I had an electrocardiograph (ECG) performed at the surgery where I was working. That confirmed that one in every three beats was what we call an ectopic beat.

I showed the ECG to a colleague who was more than a little concerned by the regular frequency of these ectopic beats. When I told him that it was my ECG, he tried to reassure me that it was something temporary and to avoid strong coffee and caffeinated drinks. I had a further ECG about a week later and nothing had changed. My own GP decided to refer me to a cardiologist. This was now late June, and the appointment came through for September of that year.

In the meantime, my family and I were on holiday in France, near Bordeaux. During our time away, I knew there was a Christian conference going on in Bordeaux and that one of the speakers was Colin Dye from London. I had previously heard Colin and knew that God used him in a healing ministry. So, as a family, we went to one of the evening services where we knew that Colin Dye was speaking. Before the time in the meeting given for preaching arrived, a young Swedish man got up to sing a song.

He introduced his song in English. He said, "I want to sing you a song entitled, 'Rise and be healed in the name of Jesus'." As he spoke those words, it was like a rama word directly to my heart! From that moment, I knew that I knew, God had healed me. A quick check after the meeting told me that my heart was now beating regularly. I went to the cardiology appointment.

A range of tests were done, including a repeat ECG, treadmill test and echocardiogram. These were all normal. A 24-hour ECG was also conducted. That was also normal. Total and complete healing. Faith for that healing came by 'a word' spoken by a Swedish singer. Over 25 years later, my heart continues to beat regularly. No more frequent ectopic beats.

Faith comes by the Name

We saw in Acts chapter three, how the lame man was healed. For as long as he could remember he had been begging. To this man, faith came as Peter and spoke the name of Jesus. Some might argue that it was the faith of Peter and John. Whilst it is true to say that, yes, they were the servants of God and yes, they spoke with authority in Jesus' Name, Peter, himself, says that faith came by the name of Jesus (Acts 3:16).

In chapter one, I shared my own experience of when I was diagnosed with cancer. It was as I prayed through the Names of God; the compound Names of God as found in the Old Testament that something began to happen. As I prayed Jehovah-Nissi (God my banner/my protector), I fell asleep. Faith came.

As I wrote in chapter one, all the Names of God are added together in the name of Jesus. Faith can come as you spend time exalting and praising God, using the name of Jesus. Philippians chapter two says:

> Let this mind be in you which was also in Christ Jesus, who, being in the form of God, did not consider it robbery to be equal with God, but made himself of no reputation, taking the form of a bondservant, and coming in the likeness of men. And being found in appearance as a man, He humbled himself and became obedient to the point of death, even the death of the cross.
> Therefore, God also has highly exalted Him and given Him the name, which is above every other name, that at the name of Jesus every knee should bow, of those in heaven, and of those on earth, and of those under the earth, and that every tongue should

confess that Jesus Christ is Lord, to the glory of God the Father. (Philippians 2:5-11)

In many of the healings in the New Testament where faith is not explicitly mentioned, it is quite possible that the sick individuals heard others speak of Jesus and of the amazing miracles that were occurring. As they began to speak to themselves the name of Jesus, could it be that something began to warm inside of them—faith was being created? Faith that caused them to step out and, even at risk to themselves (e.g. the lepers Jesus healed), to go and find Jesus.

When we pray for individuals, let us not casually add at the end of our prayer, "In Jesus' name, Amen." Rather, let us recognise the power and authority of Jesus' Name that all the Names of God are added together in that name that because of the finished work of the cross and the power of the resurrection, Jesus has all authority in heaven and on earth, and we are instructed to go in His name and heal the sick! The closing sentence of our prayer is the part that inspires faith and releases healing!

Faith comes by the Holy Spirit

In Paul's first letter to the Corinthians, in chapter twelve, he tells us that there are nine gifts of the Holy Spirit. These are gifts that can flow through any Spirit-filled Christian believer—as the Holy Spirit decides. They have nothing to do with human ability. They cannot be learned or earned! They are supernatural. All the Holy Spirit wants are willing, available vessels.

There are nine of them, but one Spirit, and it should not be surprising that in their operation, there may be some overlaps. For ease of understanding, we could place these gifts into three categories. Three vocal gifts, that is, the gift of speaking in other tongues, the gift of interpretation of tongues and the gift of prophecy.

Three revelation gifts, that is, the word of knowledge, the word of wisdom and the discerning of spirits. Then, three power gifts—the gift of healing, the gift of miracles and the gift of faith. It is the gift of faith that I want us to consider. In 1 Corinthians 12 verse nine:

> To another faith by the same Spirit.

One of my first experiences of the gift of faith was at the commencement of my pastoral ministry. In the mid-week Bible study meeting, I was doing a series of studies entitled, 'The baptism in the Spirit and the gifts of the Spirit'. This series was generating quite a lot of excitement. After teaching on the baptism in the Holy Spirit, several people had been mightily filled with the Holy Spirit. News got out about this, and new people began showing up at these mid-week meetings.

Then came the week that I was due to speak on the gift of healing. The meeting started with some songs of praise and worship and a sense of God's presence filled the room. It was at that point, I felt the Holy Spirit saying, "Pray for the sick now." My original intention had been to do that after the teaching, but I chose to do what the Holy Spirit was saying. I invited people who were sick to come forward to the front.

Several people did, including a lady I had not seen before. I felt a sense of God's anointing as I began praying for the sick. I then came to the lady that I had not seen before. She was an older lady and did not look in the best of health. As I came to her, the Holy Spirit came upon me even more powerfully, and I found myself saying to her, "You are healed in Jesus' Name."

As I laid my hand upon her, I felt the Holy Spirit flowing from me to her. It was an enormously powerful moment. I then went on to the next person, and although I still felt God's presence, it was not the same as when I prayed for the new lady.

She left immediately after the service ended. It was not until later that I found out that her name was Morfydd (a good old Welsh name) and that she suffered from several ailments, including angina, high blood pressure and heart failure. She was on several medications. When she got home, contrary to what I would have advised if I had had the opportunity to speak to her, she threw all her medication down the toilet! By the middle of the next day, she was beginning to get breathless, and her legs were beginning to swell.

Her husband was not happy! He decided to phone their GP, only to discover it was the surgery's half day and that another GP practice was covering for emergencies. He decided to wait until the next day. The next day, Morfydd got up and dressed and felt completely well. No breathlessness, no swelling.

She went for a brisk walk and, again, no breathlessness and no angina. When she was checked over by her doctor (something I would have recommended at the outset), he told her that her blood pressure was normal and there were no clinical signs of heart failure. Morfydd lived to a good old age and died of the frailty of old age.

In the meeting, I believe Morfydd received a gift of faith by the Holy Spirit. Some might say that it was a gift of healing or even a gift of miracles. It does not really matter; it is one Holy Spirit doing the work. That said, in this case, Morfydd undoubtedly received faith to keep believing even when the symptoms of her sickness began to appear.

So faith comes by the Word, by the Name and by the Spirit. Faith is a living entity, and as such, we must look after it, it needs to grow. Faith needs to be fed, faith needs to be exercised and faith needs to be confessed.

Feeding faith

Joshua received a powerful word from God, a word that created faith in his heart.

> After the death of Moses, the servant of the Lord, it came to pass that the Lord spoke to Joshua the son of Nun, Moses' assistant saying, "Moses My servant is dead. Now therefore, arise, go over this Jordan, you and all this people, to the land which am giving them—the children of Israel. Every place that the sole of your foot will tread upon have given you, as I said to Moses…" (Joshua 1:1-3)

A great word, but along with that word, God tells Joshua how he is to keep that word.

> Only be strong and very courageous, that you may observe to do all the law which Moses My servant commanded you; do not turn from it to the right hand or to the left, that you may prosper wherever you go. This Book of the Law shall not depart from your mouth, but you shall meditate in it day and night, that you may observe to do according to all that is written in it. For then you will make your way prosperous, and then you will have good success. (Joshua 1:7-8)

Joshua is encouraged to spend time in the word of God, (the Law of the Lord—that part of the Bible that was available to him), reading, memorising, meditating, and applying it. The first psalm says the same thing.

> Blessed is the man who walks not in the counsel of the ungodly, nor stands in the path of sinners, nor sits in the seat of the scornful; but his delight ins in the law of the Lord, and in His Law, he meditates day and night. (Psalm 1:1-2)

The outcome of such reading and meditation:

> He shall be like a tree planted by the rivers of water, that brings forth its fruit in its season, whose leaf also shall not wither; and whatever he does shall prosper. (Psalm 1:3)

To these quotations, we could add Psalm nineteen and Psalm one hundred and nineteen which contain further blessings and benefits of reading and meditating on God's

Word. As we read the Bible, we read of God's greatness, His love, His faithfulness, and of how He keeps His promises. Prayerful reading, meditating, and memorising of Scriptures feed our faith.

Exercising faith

If faith is to grow, it needs to be exercised. If we do not, we end up with a flabby, unhealthy faith! There are two exercises that we can apply to faith. The first exercise is praise. In Romans, chapter four, it says this of Abraham:

> He did not waver at the promise of God through unbelief, but was *strengthened* in faith, giving glory to God. (Romans 4:20)

The verse before tells us that Abraham was about one hundred years old. Sarah would be about ninety years old. God had given Abraham a very distinct faith word that he would become the father of nations. Although Abraham had made earlier mistakes, he had now come to that place in his life where he trusted the word of God. To strengthen that Word, Abraham had discovered the importance of praise—giving glory to God.

Praise is not only faith in action, but as we praise, with our eyes focussed upon God, our faith grows and is strengthened. We get a glimpse of this in 2 Chronicles chapter twenty. The small nation of Judea is surrounded by its enemies. As a nation, they are facing disaster. The king, Jehoshaphat, calls the nation to prayer. As they are praying, the Spirit of the Lord comes upon a man by the name of Jahaziel, and he prophesies:

> Listen, all you of Judah and you inhabitants of Jerusalem, and you King Jehoshaphat! Thus says the Lord to you: "Do not be afraid nor dismayed because of this great multitude, for the battle is not yours, but God's." (2 Chronicles 20:15)

He goes on to tell them what they are to do and then concludes:

> You need not to fight in this battle. Position yourselves, stand still and see the salvation of the Lord, who is with you, O Judah, and Jerusalem! Do not fear or be dismayed; tomorrow go out against them, for the Lord is with you. (2 Chronicles 20:17)

What a word! The king and the people worship the Lord. But what about the next day? It is so easy to receive a word from God, be all excited about it, have a night's sleep, then wake up seeing the problem is still out there and begin to doubt. Not Jehoshaphat and his people. They had learned that praise causes faith to grow and be activated. The king says to the people:

> "Believe in the Lord your God, and you shall be established; believe His prophets, and you shall prosper." And when he had consulted with the people, he appointed those who should sing to the Lord, and who should praise the beauty of holiness, as they went out before the army and were saying: "Praise the Lord, for His mercy endures for ever."

> Now when they began to sing and to praise, the Lord set ambushes against the enemies; and they were defeated. (2 Chronicles 20:20-22)

When we receive a word from God, we need to praise Him for that word. Our faith grows stronger when we praise Him.

The second exercise for our faith is prayer. In the penultimate book of the Bible, the book of Jude, Jude writes:

> But you, beloved, building yourselves up on your most holy faith, praying in the Holy Spirit. (Jude:20)

When God gives us, a faith-creating word, our response should be to pray over that word. Thanking Him for it, praising Him that His word cannot fail, that He is a faithful God. So often, in prayer, we fire off several requests in the hope that one will hit the target, adding an 'If it is your will' at the end.

What a different story it is when we have a word from God. We then know what His will is, and we can then pray powerfully and effectively. When we are not sure what words to use, Jude's advice is, 'Pray in the Spirit'.

When a believer is mightily baptised in the Holy Spirit, an accompanying sign is the ability to speak in other tongues—known and unknown languages given by the Spirit. There are those who have wondered what the point of this is. Well, there are several reasons, and one of them is that we might pray in the Spirit.

When Jesus was on earth, He spent much time in communion with His Father, going from one place of prayer to another place of prayer and in between working miracles and teaching the people with authority. Now the Holy Spirit has come. He too has a great desire for prayer. We, as temples of the Holy Spirit, are the vessels through whom He wants to pray. In Romans, chapter 8, Paul writes:

> Likewise, the Spirit also helps in our weaknesses. For we do not know what we should pray for as we ought, but the Spirit Himself makes intercession for us with groanings which cannot be uttered. Now He who searches the hearts knows what the mind of the Spirit is, because He makes intercession for the saints according to the will of God. (Romans 8:26-27)

Paul, the Apostle, knew what it was to spend much time praying in the Spirit (1 Corinthians 14:18). When you consider all the churches, fellow workers, and new believers he had in his heart, then I am quite sure that he was grateful for the help of the Holy Spirit. As Jude says, praying in the Spirit builds up our faith.

Confessing faith

In his letter, James says:

> For as the body without the spirit is dead, so faith without works is dead also. (James 3:26)

Faith needs to be confessed and acted upon. We see this with regard to salvation.

> If you confess with your mouth the Lord Jesus and believe in your heart that God has raised Him from the dead, you will be saved. (Romans 10:9)

What is true for salvation is true for healing. When we receive faith (by the Word, by the Name or by the Holy Spirit), then we need to confess/declare that—in prayer, praise and in the company of people of faith. Faith needs to be expressed in an atmosphere of faith with people who affirm and encourage our God-given faith. In Hebrews chapter eleven, the writer gives us a list of people of faith. As he starts the next chapter, he writes:

> Therefore, we also, since we are surrounded by so great a cloud of witnesses, let us lay aside every weight, and the sin which so easily ensnares us, and let us run with endurance the race that is set before us, looking unto Jesus, the author and finisher of our faith. (Hebrews 12:1-2)

The Hebrew's eleven list of Old Testament people of faith is given to encourage us as we live our life of faith, looking unto Jesus, who is the author and finisher of faith. If we surround ourselves with the wrong people, people who are sceptical and negative, then that will be detrimental to faith. Conversely, if we surround ourselves with people of faith, who stand with us, pray with us, and encourage us, then in that environment of faith, faith flourishes and faith grows!

As a young Christian, I remember hearing the story of a lady who had a large goitre (thyroid swelling) to her neck. This lady had gone forward for prayer and had felt God's touch in a powerful way (received a gift of faith by the Holy Spirit). From that moment on she began to thank God for her healing. In open times of prayer in the church services, she would thank God for her healing. The only problem was the large goitre swelling was still present.

To some in the church, her prayers became an embarrassment. Eventually, they spoke to the minister and asked him to talk to the lady and ask her to refrain from praying. The minister, with some reluctance, did so. The response of the lady was to at the next opportunity pray, "Lord, you have healed me. I know you have healed me. Now show them you have healed me!" Immediately, the goitre disappeared!

The elephant in the room

I enjoy writing and speaking about faith, but I am also aware there are situations where people have not been healed, despite them having a word from God and despite them giving thanks and praising God. Well, such people are in good company. Hebrews chapter eleven says:

> By faith Abraham obeyed when he was called to go out to the place which he would receive as an inheritance. And he went out, not knowing where he was going. By faith he dwelt in the land of promise as in a foreign country, dwelling in tents with Isaac and Jacob, the heirs with him of the same promise: for he waited for the city, whose builder and maker is God. (Hebrews 11:8-10)

Did Abraham arrive at the Divinely built city in his lifetime? No. But he continued believing and continued praising (Romans 4:20). The writer to Hebrews continues:

> These all died in faith, not having received the promises but having seen them afar off were assured of them, embraced them, and confessed that they were strangers and pilgrims on the earth. For those who say such things declare plainly that they seek a homeland. And truly if they had called to mind that country from which they had come out, they would have had opportunity to return. But now they desire a better, that is, a heavenly country. Therefore, God is not ashamed to be called their God, for He has prepared a city for them. (Hebrews 11:13-16)

Earlier, the writer to Hebrews says, regarding Enoch:

By faith Enoch was taken away so that he did not see death, "and was not found because God had taken him," for before he was taken, he had this testimony that he pleased God. But without faith it is impossible to please Him, for he who comes to God must believe that He is, and that He is a rewarder of those who diligently seek Him. (Hebrews 11:5-6)

Note that faith pleases God. When we have received a word from God, when faith has been given, then, as we keep praising, keep believing, keep confessing, even up to our dying breath that pleases God. Yes, of course, we use those things that God has made available to us, through medicine and surgery, to ease our sickness and suffering, but we keep looking to Him, trusting and believing.

At the end of the day, this life is but a vapour. Eternity awaits—and for the Christian believer that means no sickness, no pain, and an incorruptible, immortal body. The ultimate healing! In the interim, let us keep believing—faith pleases God.

Chapter 5
Three Parts Whole

She felt that her life was wasting away. For twelve years she had suffered from menorrhagia—heavy, persistent menstrual bleeding. This was draining. She was getting progressively more and more anaemic, weak, and tired. Her financial resources were also drained. She had spent all her savings visiting various physicians.

If that were not bad enough, she lived in a culture that said that a woman with such a condition was 'unclean' and could not mix with other people.[9] Twelve years of loneliness and social deprivation. To say that she felt depressed was an understatement. To add to her physical and mental state, she felt cut off from God.

Into that physical suffering and loneliness, shone a glimmer of hope. She could hear people talking about a man called Jesus. She could detect the excitement in their voices as they spoke of the lame walking, the blind seeing, the deaf hearing and the dumb speaking. As she began to speak that name, Jesus, to herself, faith began to arise in her heart.

---

[9] Leviticus 15:19-27.

She thought to herself, *If I could just touch the hem of his garment, then I, too, could be healed. Yes, it is risky. I know I am not supposed to mix with other people, but if I cover myself and just reach out to his garment from behind, and then quickly leave, non-one will know.*

Luke, in his Gospel, picks up the story:

> Now a woman came from behind and touched the border of His garment. And immediately her flow of blood stopped. And Jesus said, "Who touched me?" When all denied it, Peter, and those with him said, "Master, the multitudes throng and press You, and You say, 'Who touched me?'" But Jesus said, "Somebody touched Me, for I perceived power going out from Me."
>
> Now when the woman saw that she was not hidden, she came trembling; and falling down before Him, she declared to Him in the presence of all the people the reason she had touched Him and how she was healed immediately. And He said to her, "Daughter, be of good cheer; your faith has made you well. Go in peace." (Luke 8:43-48)

The translation for 'your faith has made you well' can equally be, 'your faith has made you whole'. [10] Whole—body, soul, and spirit.

In an earlier chapter, I mentioned that we are created in the image of God. Genesis, chapter one, says:

---

[10] Young's Analytical Concordance of the Bible, KJV, page 1050.

> Then God said, "Let Us make man in Our image, according to our likeness." (Genesis 1:26)

There are many things that we could learn from this statement. The one that I want to address now is that God is three beings, yet one. Father, Son, and Holy Spirit, yet one God. "Let Us make man in Our image, according to Our likeness." So God created man in His own image (Genesis 1:27). How does that affect us? Well, created in the image of God, we are three-part beings, yet one. In his first letter to the Thessalonians, Paul writes:

> Now may the God of peace sanctify you completely; and may your whole spirit, soul, and body be preserved blameless at the coming of our Lord Jesus Christ. (1 Thessalonians 5:23)

There we have it, spirit, soul, and body—yet one being. Note the order. We tend to start from the body and work inwards. God starts from the spirit and works outwards. Let us define each part.

We will do it in the human order! So we start with the body, the physical part of our being, and the part of our being we concentrate on the most. Hygiene, cleanliness, appearance, fitness, and diet are just a few of the things that come to mind when we start thinking of the body. When we think of illness and disease, we tend to primarily think of the effects on the body, but we are more than physical beings.

We also have a soul. It can be difficult to define the soul. Yes, it includes our minds and our emotions, but also reflects our innermost being, the part of us that gives us individuality and personality. The body has a beginning and an end—we are born, we age, we die.

The soul has a beginning but no end. The soul does not age in the same way as the body—ever wondered why part of you still feels young, even if your body is beginning to creak? Let me illustrate further.

Suppose that when you were young, you had a close friend at university. You were almost inseparable. You laughed and joked together; you understood what made the other tick. Then, just imagine, you went your separate ways. The years rolled by, and you had had no contact with each other.

Then, after many years you bump into an old acquaintance. They talk about your one-time friend and inform you that he is now seriously ill with cancer. You get details of where he is living and determine to see him. When you arrive at his home, you are shocked to see him. Not only has he aged (as have you), but he has been seriously affected by the ravages of cancer.

His hair has fallen out, his face is gaunt, his once powerful limbs are like match sticks, and his abdomen is swollen. Physically, you would never have recognised him. He asks you in, and then you begin to talk, reminisce, and even joke. Something shines out from the wrecked body, something that tells you that without doubt, this is your one-time close friend. That, I suggest, is the soul. That part of us that makes me, me, and you, you.

I have often been asked, "How will we recognise one another in heaven, seeing that we have new glorified bodies?" Obviously, our new glorified bodies will have abilities and capacities that we do not currently have. That said, we will be able to recognise one another by our souls. We get a glimpse of this in the Mount of Transfiguration story (Matthew 17:1-8). Jesus, along with Peter, James and John goes up the mountain, and on that mountain, Jesus is transfigured—his face shines like the sun and his clothes become as white as light. Then there appear Moses and Elijah, talking with Him.

There are many things we can learn from this event, but what I want us to notice is that Peter recognised Moses and Elijah. Maybe they were introduced but remembering that both Moses and Elijah were in heaven, Peter was, nonetheless able to recognise them. So will we, after the resurrection (or rapture) of believers.

Then, the third part of our three-part being is our spirit. This is the God-conscious part of our being. In Genesis chapter two, it says:

> And the Lord God formed man of the dust of the ground and breathed into his nostrils the breath of life: and the man became a living being. (Genesis 2:7)

From that moment on, Adam was able to commune with God, who is Spirit, experiencing the glorious presence of God. Of course, that was all messed up by the fall of man. Sin became a barrier between man's spirit man and God. That is, until Jesus came and died in our place upon the cross. Through faith in His substitutionary sacrifice, our spirit man can come alive again and experience God. Paul writes to the Ephesians:

> You He made alive, who were dead in trespasses and sins. (Ephesians 2:1)

Here, he is writing of the spirit man coming alive. From that moment onwards, we can begin to worship God in spirit and truth.

> But the hour is coming, and now is, when the true worshippers will worship the Father in spirit and truth: for the Father is seeking such to worship Him. God is Spirit, and those who worship Him must worship in spirit and truth. (John 4:23-24)

The Westminster Catechism, written in 1646 and 1647, by a synod of English and Scottish theologians, states, "Man's chief end is to glorify God and enjoy Him forever." When our spirit man is set free, then we can enter into worship as never before, experiencing God, sensing His peace and presence and finding ourselves 'lost in wonder, love and praise'.

Whilst it is great to engage our minds in worship and sing Christian songs, there is another level where our spirit engages God. As a non-musician, I love it, when my whole being is engaged in the worship of God. It is a place of beautiful intimacy with God, where heaven touches earth, and I am lost in God's presence. This is what was happening to the church at Antioch when Luke writes:

> As they ministered to the Lord and fasted, the Holy Spirit said, "Now separate to Me Barnabas and Saul for the work to which I have called them." (Acts 13:2)

The church was loving God, worshipping God, and became so lost in His presence that two things happened—they forgot all about food and fasted, and their hearts began to beat with the heartbeat of God and the prophetic voice of the Holy Spirit was heard. The spirit part of their beings was to the fore.

Three parts being, but one. Why is this important? Well, understanding this can have a significant impact not only on understanding sickness and receiving healing, but ministering healing to others. It is well-known by doctors that chronic illness has an impact on a patient's mental health. When we, or our specialist nurses, were reviewing patients with conditions such as chronic obstructive airway disease or diabetes, included in the review were questions related to their mental well-being.

The same could be said for other chronic conditions. In the language of us being a three-part being, the physical illness could be affecting the soul of the patient. Put the other way round, someone who is suffering from depression/low mood is more likely to develop physical illness—and they are less likely to want to pray! The good news is, if we can begin to minister to one of the areas of the three-part being, then that is going to affect the other two areas. Consider the following scenarios.

You are feeling low in mood. You do not want to pray. A friend drops by and tells you that they are going to take you out for the day. They take you to a beautiful place in the countryside. You go for a walk together.

The scenery is amazing, the fresh air is invigorating, the exercise is stimulating, and the conversation is uplifting. You begin to feel uplifted. You want to worship. What is happening? It is the beautiful interaction of body, soul, and spirit.

Another scenario. You have a physical illness, and it's beginning to get you down. You put on some worship music. As the music plays and you listen to the words of the music songs, something begins to stir within you.

In time, you begin to join in with the songs, you begin to raise your hands in worship to God, and as you do, you sense the Holy Spirit ministering to your whole being. What is happening? The spirit part of your being is uplifted and begins to affect your soul and body.

I love the Hebrew word for peace—shalom. It is more than the absence of conflict or distress. Shalom contains the thought of wholeness, blessing, and prosperity. Jesus may well have used 'shalom' in addressing the lady mentioned at the beginning of this chapter. "Go in peace (shalom)." 'Shalom' is used in the priestly blessing:

> The Lord bless you and keep you; the Lord make His face shine upon you and be gracious to you; the Lord lift up His countenance upon you and give you peace (shalom). (Numbers 6:24-26)

In ministry, someone may come forward for prayer with an obvious physical need. However, as we (the ones who are ministering) are sensitive to the Holy Spirit, it could well be that before we can minister to the physical need there is an area of the soul or spirit that needs ministering to first.

As a young GP, one night, I was called out to a terminally ill patient who had been getting increasingly short of breath. She had advanced cancer which, by this time, had infiltrated her lungs. It was her desire to die at home, so the option of admitting her to the hospital was not available. Other options included using sedatives or increasing her morphine. As I weighed up these options, I felt the Holy Spirit telling me that her real problem was a lack of peace in her soul.

Gently, I put this to her. "You are very breathless, and I know this is, in itself, very distressing, but I sense there may be something else troubling you. Am I right?" It was difficult for her to speak because of the breathlessness, but she nodded her head and tears began to flow. I went on, "What I sense is that you want peace?" Again, she nodded—this time with the look of a plea upon her face, as if to say, "Yes, please!" I then told her that as well as being a doctor, I was a Christian minister. I asked if I could pray for her.

Again, she readily agreed, by nodding. I prayed a prayer and then invited her to pray with me (I would pray the words and she would quietly herself, pray the same words). I prayed for her to receive the peace of God and she followed me in a prayer inviting Jesus, the Prince of Peace, into her heart and life.

When we finished praying, a peace came over her. She was still breathless but not as much as before. She, by the look on her face, was extremely grateful for what had just happened. Some hours later, she peacefully passed away.

How important it is to listen to the promptings of the Holy Spirit!

Chapter 6
Healing of the Soul

In the last chapter, we defined the soul in terms of the mind, the emotions, the will, the conscience, and the personality. We said that it is the soul that gives us our individual uniqueness. No one else in the whole wide world is like me! The Greek word for the soul is 'psuche' from which we get the English word 'psyche'.

Vine, in his expository dictionary of New Testament words, looks at the various ways in which the word 'psuche' is used in the New Testament.[11] He says that it is used with reference to the immaterial, the invisible part of man, the disembodied man, the seat of the personality, the seat of the sentiment element in man, that by which we perceive, reflect, feel, desire, the seat of the will and purpose, and the inward man.

In whatever way we try and define and understand the soul, it is not difficult to see how the soul can be damaged and bruised. By referring to a Bible concordance and looking up references to the soul, one can discover an extensive list of

---

[11] Vine's Complete Expository Dictionary of Old and New Testament Words, W. E. Vine, Thomas Nelson.

ways in which the soul can be afflicted.[12] A few of those references from the Bible include bitterness of the soul, vexation of the soul, weariness of the soul, grieving of the soul, restoration of the soul, humbling of the soul, and healing of the soul. The soul can be cast down, broken and sorrowful.

Rejection, guilt, and grief have their primary effect on the area of the soul. Along with them, and arising from them, we have inferiority, insecurity, depression, fears, and anxiety states. The soul can be afflicted in a very real, and at times, disabling way.

In this regard, they are no different to someone suffering from a physical condition, such as arthritis, heart disease or cancer, and they require just as much care, compassion and understanding in their treatment. Sadly, even in Christian circles, that is not always the case. We shall explore some cases that I have dealt with, to help us get a better understanding of these 'afflictions of the soul'.

The first case is of a young married woman whom we shall call Jane (not her real name). When Jane came to see me, her face was almost expressionless, and she sat down in a tired, kind of mechanical way. She looked pale and tired. When invited to share why she had come to see me, she found it very hard to express, in words, what she was feeling. It wasn't long before she filled up with tears and began to cry.

I passed her an open box of paper handkerchiefs. This is a valuable, non-verbal way of saying, "Don't be embarrassed about crying."

After a few more moments, she sufficiently regained her composure, to be able to begin to tell me how she felt.

---

[12] Analytical Concordance of the Bible, Young, Lutterworth Press.

"Doctor, I can't cope. I don't feel like doing any housework or doing anything at all. My husband and children are wonderful, but I don't feel anything for them. In fact, I've lost all feeling of feelings. I'm awake almost all night, just thinking. I don't see the point of carrying on anymore. I might as well be dead."

Each of these statements came out between sobs and more tears. After summarising and repeating some of the things, she had just said (to show that I was listening), I proceeded to ask her some questions about her family and about her past. It was, as I gained her confidence, that she began to tell me about a relationship that she had had before marrying her husband. It had been a short-lived relationship, little more than 'a one-night stand'.

As a result of this sexual encounter, she had become pregnant. Her boyfriend finished with her, and she went to a private clinic for a termination of the pregnancy. Now, it seemed, years later, the guilt of all that had happened still haunted her, reducing her to this state of depression.

She felt better for talking and bringing to light something that had happened many years before. The consultation had been longer than usual but had been necessary in order to begin to unravel what was going on in Jane's life. I arranged to see her again.

Medically, what had happened could be summed up in words, such as, 'Reactive depression. Management—counselling'. However, spiritually, there was no doubt in my mind; Jane had an affliction of the soul. Depression resulting from the guilt of unconfessed sin. The best course of action, for Jane, would have been for someone to share God's love and forgiveness with her, and for her to receive the total cleansing of her sin, a right relationship with God, and wholeness through Jesus.

As doctors, we are constrained as to what we can and cannot do. In situations like this, it is so helpful to have a chaplaincy service operating alongside a GP surgery and to be able to offer that service, as well as the usual counselling services. In some areas there are Christian-run pregnancy counselling services that sensitively and compassionately help someone like Jane.[13] As many as a quarter of women (some studies say more, depending on how depression and mental health are reported)[14] who have had a termination of pregnancy experience some degree of depression and for a few, like Jane, continue to suffer from depression even years later.

Another case I was involved with, some years ago, involved a man from another congregation. His name was John, and he was referred to me by his own church minister. He presented to me, together with his wife and his minister. John's wife and the minister initially spoke for John.

The story was that John had become increasingly anxious and irritable. He had been prescribed some tranquillisers, but other than making him drowsy, were doing nothing to alleviate his problem.

John, himself, felt very insecure. He felt that his wife was going to leave him that his children didn't love him, and no one at the church cared for him. He felt that he had to try and

---

[13] Example: The Willow Tree Centre, Yate. www.thewillowtreecentre.org.uk.

[14] Abortion and Mental Health, *The British Journal of Psychiatry*, Volume 199, Issue 3.

constantly prove to other church members that he wanted to be friendly. Despite having a genuine experience of salvation, he was terrified that God would cast him off. The minister, John's wife, and most of all, John himself, were keen for something to be done.

I began by getting John's story. From a medical perspective, this included going back to John's childhood. In doing so, a significant picture emerged. John was the youngest child in a family where there were ten children in all.

Owing to the size of the family, and John being the youngest, he was cared for by older siblings and close relatives. His first memories of childhood were of being passed from one relative to another. He could not recall developing a deep or close relationship with his own parents. His only recollection was one of feeling unwanted and insecure.

It became clear to me, that what had happened to John as a child, was now affecting the way that he behaved as an adult. I explained this to John, and he was able to see the link. I then suggested to John that this was a condition of the soul, and although counselling could be beneficial, healing prayer, in the name of Jesus, was the way forward. Healing of the memories of his childhood that had left their scars upon his adult life. He agreed and we spent some time in prayer.

I asked the Lord to heal him of the rejection and insecurity that afflicted his innermost being—his soul. I prayed for every emotional scar to be removed. After prayer, I encouraged John and his wife to talk through what we had discovered. I encouraged John to meditate on God's unfailing love and Fatherhood. It is when we are secure in the love of God that we can engage in meaningful relationships with others, without fear of rejection.

John's case is not unique. The world is full of troubled adults who have emotional scars left over from their childhood. Whilst I write, I am well aware that there are children growing up in an environment of rejection and insecurity. Homes where hate replaces love, where couples constantly fight and there is daily abuse and violence. Where children live in fear of an alcoholic parent or come home from school to an empty home.

Then there are those parents who lavish their children with expensive toys in order to appease their own guilt, of not spending quality time with the children. Add to a dysfunctional home life an intimidating, bullying peer group, and it doesn't take much imagination to recognise the crippling effect this had on a child's emotional development. Scars will manifest in later years through emotional disorders, insecurity, violent outrages, fears and anxiety states.

For many years, I had the privilege of working alongside Teen Challenge UK, as a director on its Board of Directors. Teen Challenge is a Christian organisation seeking to help those with life-controlling drug and alcohol problems. When speaking about drug addiction, I would often say, "Drugs are just the symptom of a deeper problem. As you dig deeper, more often than nought, you will discover dysfunction that goes all the way back to childhood."

A Scottish Health Education Poster, I once read, said:

> If a child lives with criticism,
> She learns to condemn.
> If a child lives with hostility,

He learns to fight.
If a child lives with ridicule,
She learns to be shy.
If a child lives with shame,
He learns to feel guilt.
If a child lives with tolerance,
She learns to be patient.
If a child lives with encouragement,
He learns confidence.
If a child lives with praise,
She learns to appreciate.
If a child lives with fairness,
He learns justice.
If a child lives with security,
She learns to have faith.
If a child lives with approval,
He learns to like himself.
If a child lives with acceptance and friendship,
He or she learns to find love in the world.[15]

Thank God, there is healing for our soul. The Psalmist could pray, "Heal my soul" (Psalm 41:4). Peter, in his first epistle, tells us that Jesus is the shepherd and overseer of our souls. (1 Peter 2:25).

Like the shepherds of old moving in and out of their sheep, anointing their wounds with oil, removing thorns, and caressing their woolly necks, so Jesus anoints and heals our wounded souls. He removes the thorns of the past and causes us to stand secure in His love. What we need to be aware of is

---

[15] Children learn what they live. Poem by Dorothy Law Nolte.

that ministering to those with 'afflictions of the soul' is usually not a one-session-fix-all ministry.

It may take repeated sessions of ministry, loving counsel, prayer, and Biblical affirmation before the individual begins to feel whole again. They, like all of us, need to daily remind ourselves of who we are in Christ. Paul in the first chapter of his Ephesian Epistle, says:

> Blessed be the God and Father of our Lord Jesus Christ, who has blessed us with every spiritual blessing in the heavenly places in Christ. (Ephesians 1:3)

"Note that He has blessed us. This is not some future blessing; it is for now! Paul goes on to list the blessings that are ours. In verse four, he says that 'we are chosen'; in verse five, 'we are adopted as sons'; in verse six, 'we are accepted"; in verse seven, 'we are redeemed'; and in verse thirteen, 'we are sealed with the Holy Spirit' (the mark of Divine ownership). I regularly go through these blessings in my own devotional times with the Lord. He loves me and has chosen me.

He has made me His child and I can call Him 'Abba, Father' (Romans 8:15, Galatians 4:6). Irrespective of my past, I am accepted. I have been purchased by His precious blood and set free from the bondage of sin and death; I am redeemed. He has filled me and empowered me with His Holy Spirit; I am sealed by the Spirit. Confessing these blessings reaffirms my security in Christ and 'strengthens my soul'.

Guilt

If rejection and insecurity are one way that the soul can be afflicted, then guilt is another. We saw in Jane's case how guilt can reduce a person to a sad state of depression. In such instances, tranquillisers and antidepressants have little, or no effect. The root cause must be dealt with.

On one occasion I was helping out another doctor. A lady came to see me who was suffering from insomnia. She was already taking a hefty dose of antidepressants and sleeping tablets. Despite the medication, and despite following sleep guidance sheets, she was still not getting a good night's sleep.

As we talked together, I asked her how long she had been in this state. She said that she had been like this for forty years. As she was quite clear about the time, I asked her what had been going on in her life at that time. It was then that the story emerged.

She told me that her first and only child had been born with a severe heart condition. The child required lots of attention and there had been several occasions when she had nursed him back from the edge of death. When he was ten years old, she was told about a new operation that could benefit her son's heart condition. Without the operation, his prognosis was very poor, with it, there was the possibility of living a normal life.

However, there was still a significant mortality rate with this new surgery. It was a difficult decision for her to make, but eventually, she decided to have the surgery done. Fourteen children were operated on at the same time as her son. Six of them died, her son being one of them. He never regained consciousness after the operation.

It was from that day on that this mother was overcome with guilt. She blamed herself for her son's death. Forty years later that guilt complex was still manifesting itself as severe insomnia. Drugs were not her answer.

Her real need was healing of her soul, healing of the memory of the past, and removal of the guilt. I discovered that this lady was a Christian and was able to briefly share my thoughts with her, encouraging her to go and speak to her own minister. She did. On the last occasion I saw her, she was much better—having received spiritual help.

Guilt is a great crippler. We can try and cover it up, seek to justify ourselves and our actions, but all of the time it is like cancer eroding away at our very soul, until eventually our whole being is overcome by it. It is only as the Holy Spirit uncovers it, and we turn our lives over to God at the foot of the cross that we can receive total forgiveness through Jesus Christ. In the words of the hymn writer:

> There is a fountain filled with blood
> Drawn from Immanuel's veins
> And sinners plunged beneath that flood,
> Lose all their guilty stains.

I have found that before a person will open up about issues such as guilt, we have to build trust and confidence. That can take some time, but once established, frees the way for the guilt problem to be talked about. We then need to follow the leading of the Holy Spirit, the Great Counsellor, as to when to bring the person to a place of repentance, forgiveness, and healing.

This sequence is clearly illustrated in an incident in the life of King David. It is recorded for us in the second book of Samuel, chapters eleven and twelve. We read that it was the time of year that kings went out to battle (a modern-day equivalent could be the Rugby Six Nations Tournament). David should have been one of those kings, but on this occasion, he decided to stay at home and sent Joab, his commander-in-chief, to take his place.

With all the men out fighting, a beautiful woman by the name of Bathsheba decides to have a relaxing bath on her rooftop balcony. From his vantage point in the palace, David sees her. Before he knows it, his mind becomes preoccupied with lustful thoughts for this woman. He invites her to the palace and ends up committing adultery with her.

Bathsheba finds herself pregnant, and David, in an effort to cover up his sin, calls Bathsheba's husband, Uriah, home from the battlefield. Despite David's best efforts, Uriah remains loyal to the last and refuses to take the opportunity to go home and sleep with his wife. Uriah was keen to get back to the battlefield and fight for his king!

Realising that his scheme was not working, David arranges for Uriah to go back to the battlefield. Orders accompany Uriah for him to be positioned where the fighting is the heaviest, and at a strategic moment, the rest of the army is to be pulled back, exposing Uriah to the enemy and to a certain death on the battlefield. This time David's deadly scheme, works. A messenger informs David that Uriah has died on the battlefield.

After a discrete mourning period, Bathsheba is married to David. Initially, David might have felt pleased with himself that he had managed to cover up his sin but that feeling didn't last very long. Outwardly he may have looked no different, but deep in his soul, guilt feelings began to gnaw away at him—affecting his physical being. The man who once lived for God now found the heavens as brass.

> When I kept silent, my bones grew old through my groaning all day long. For day and night Your hand was heavy upon me; my vitality was turned into the drought of summer. (Psalm 32:3-4)
> If I regard iniquity in my heart, the Lord will not hear. (Psalm 66:18)

The joy of his salvation was replaced by guilt. It is at this point that God, the all-seeing, the all-knowing God, sends Nathan the prophet to David.

It is worth noting that Nathan doesn't come with a sledgehammer to crush David into the ground, but rather brings David to a place where the deep feelings of his soul are aroused, and the sin and guilt exposed. Nathan's Divinely guided method of doing this is by means of a parable (2 Samuel 12:1-4). A combination of a word of wisdom and a word of knowledge. The parable is about a poor man whose only possession was a cherished ewe lamb that he and his family treated as a pet, and about a rich man who had everything.

When the rich man has a friend come to stay. He decides to put on a banquet for his friend. Without any feeling for the poor man, the rich man takes the poor man's ewe lamb and has it cooked for his banquet.

This parable arouses deep feelings within David's soul, and, in anger, he turns to Nathan, and says, "As the Lord lives, the man who has done this thing shall surely die! And he shall restore fourfold for the lamb because he did this thing and because he had no pity" (2 Samuel 12:5).

Then Nathan says to David, "You are the man!" With further words (2 Samuel 12:7-14), Nathan goes on to describe David's sin, and God's reaction to that sin. David cries in repentance before the Lord. Psalm fifty-one expresses his repentance.

> Have mercy upon me, O God, according to your loving-kindness; according to the multitude of your tender mercies, blot out my transgressions. Wash me thoroughly from my iniquity and cleanse me from my sin.
> Against you, and you only, I have sinned, and done this evil in your sight.
> Purge me with hyssop and I shall be clean; wash me, and I shall be whiter than snow.
> Hide your face from my sins, and blot out all my iniquities. Create in me a clean heart, o God, and renew a steadfast spirit within me. (Psalm 51:1-2, 4, 7, 9-10)

In this story, we see something of the beautiful way in which justice and mercy are balanced. God is never pleased with sin, but as He looks at the sin and guilt-stricken heart, He longs that the sin be dealt with, confessed and repented of, so that the relationship with Himself can be restored. Following his heart-felt repentance, David had the assurance that his sin had been forgiven. In Psalm one hundred and three, David praises God by saying:

> Bless the Lord, O my soul; and all that is within me, bless His Holy name! Bless the Lord, O my soul, and forget not all His benefits: who forgives all your iniquities, who heals all your diseases, who redeems your life from destruction, who crowns you with loving-kindness and tender mercies, who satisfies your mouth with good things, so that your youth is renewed like the eagle's.
>
> As far as the east is from the west, so far as He removed our transgressions from us. (Psalm 103:1-5, 12)

As we follow this story of David's sin and guilt and how he is brought to repentance, it reinforces our need for the help of the Holy Spirit in dealing with the sensitive and deep issues afflicting a person's soul. Later in this book, we look at words of wisdom and knowledge—and they are certainly required in this area. Repentance is certainly vital to a good outcome. Thanksgiving and praise for God's love and forgiveness are important in maintaining victory over past sin and guilt. When Christ bore our sins on Calvary's tree, He did so, once and for all. May our souls truly magnify the Lord!

Chapter 7
Overcoming the Blues

Have you ever experienced feeling low mood, being tearful, being not motivated, having no concentration, having no drive, and generally feeling that life is not worth living? You have lost the feeling of feelings. You've either been eating too much (comfort eating) or not bothered eating at all. Your personal appearance has taken a nosedive. Your sleep is disturbed. Mixing with people is the last thing you want to do.

You just want to be left alone. If you have—and it lasts more than two weeks, then you have been suffering from depression. Obviously, there are degrees of depression. Those who are experiencing extremely dark and suicidal thoughts are going to need psychiatric help and treatment. There is a scoring system for depression called the PHQ-9.

This consists of nine questions which you answer by scoring 0 for not at all, 1 for several days, 2 for more than half the days and 3 for nearly every day. A score of 0-5 is mild depression, 6-10 moderate depression, 11-15 moderately severe and 16-20 severe depression[16]. In this chapter, we are

---

[16] Devon Partnership NHS Trust www.dpt.nhs.uk Appendix B: PHQ-9-7 GAD.

going to look at the less severe end of the spectrum, where, from time to time, many of us may find ourselves.

To help us, I am going to take you to a 'virtual psychiatric clinic'. We have three patients to see, with many more on the waiting list. All three have suffered from depression and all three have overcome it. Their names may surprise you. They are David, Elijah, and Paul. Yes, David the giant slayer, Elijah who called down fire from heaven, and Paul the Apostle and great church planter extraordinaire!

David

In his life, David knew great highs and great lows. Slaying Goliath was certainly a great high—although his heart must have been pounding and his mouth dry as he took aim with his sling at the advancing battle-trained giant! When people had said, "He's too big to hit." It had been easy to reply, "He's too big to miss!" In the heat of battle, it was another thing. David's eyes were focussed on God.

> You come to me with a sword, with a spear, and with a javelin. But I come to you in the name of the Lord of hosts, the God of the armies of Israel, whom you have defied. This day the Lord will deliver you into my hand, and I will strike you and take your head from you. (1 Samuel 17:45-46)

Yes, slaying Goliath had been a high. But there had been some lows. Lows, such as, when King Saul, out of jealousy, tries to kill David—forcing David to go into hiding. Lows, such as, when David's own son, Absalom, commits treason, and forces David, who was then Israel's king, to flee Jerusalem and go into hiding. It was out of this experience that Psalm forty-two is penned.

> As the deer pants for the water brooks, so pants my soul for You, O God. My soul thirsts for God, for the living God. When shall I come and appear before God? My tears have been my food day and night, whilst they continually say to me, "Where is your God?"
> When I remember these things, I pour out my soul within me. For I used to go with the multitude; I went with them to the house of God, with my voice of joy and praise, with a multitude that kept a pilgrim feast. Why are you cast down, O my soul? And why are you disquieted within me? (Psalm 42:1-5a)

In the opening verse, David likens himself to a hunted deer. Chased out of its normal habitat by the hunter, the deer is frightened, its heart pounding and its mouth dry. It pants for water, desperate for a refreshing drink and an opportunity to reacclimatise and make its escape. This is how David feels, except he is not panting for water, but thirsting for God and God's presence. To add to his discomfort, he hears the voice of people jeering and mocking, "Where's God now?" At a time when David needs to hear words of encouragement and affirmation, he is, instead, bombarded with negative words which generate doubt and make him paranoid (feels that people are out to get him).

He is cut off, paranoid, isolated, agitated, restless, not eating, and tearful. He says, "My tears have been my food day and night." He longs for the past—the good times—but sees no way back there. Then comes the statement, confirming his depression, "Why are you cast down, o my soul? And why are you disquieted within me?" Deep within his mind and his emotions, he feels low. Hopeless, helpless, and cast off. David was depressed. Yes, the faith-filled giant slayer was depressed.

Did he stay depressed? No. So how did he get out of the depression? The clues are in the psalm. David starts speaking to himself.

> Why are you cast down, O my soul? And why are you disquieted within me? Hope in God, for I shall yet praise Him for the help of His countenance.
> O my God, my soul is cast down within me: therefore, I will remember You from the land of the Jordan, and from the heights of Hermon, from the hills of Mizar. Deep calls unto deep at the noise of Your waterfalls; all Your waves and billows have gone over me. The Lord will command His loving-kindness in the daytime, and in the night His song shall be with me—a prayer to the God of my life.
> I will say to God my rock, "Why have You forgotten me? Why do I go mourning because of the oppression of my enemy?" As with a breaking of my bones, my enemies reproach me, whilst they say to me all day long, "Where is your God?"

Why are you cast down, O my soul? And why are you disquieted within me? Hope in God; for I will yet praise Him, the help of my countenance and my God.

As David speaks to himself, he decides to focus on God and what God has done. As he reviews his past, he can confidently say, "The Lord will command His lovingkindness in the daytime, and in the night His song shall be with me." What an important lesson to us—to review our past and remember God's faithfulness.

Better still, keep a journal and highlight God's blessing, God's provisions, and God's faithfulness. Something else that I do, is to use colouring crayons to colour in Scriptures in my Bible. Verses that have spoken to me, blessed me and inspired me, I colour in yellow. When I am feeling under the weather, I can open my Bible—usually to the psalms—and just start reading these highlighted verses.

David's review of his past and reminding himself of all that God has done causes him to speak to his soul, and say, "Hope in God." From that point, David begins to praise God. "I shall yet praise Him for the help of His countenance."

Whatever our circumstances may look like, praising God is vital. Time and time again, in Scripture, we find that praise releases God's power and presence (consider 2 Chronicles 20:21-22, Acts 16:23-26). To a nation that had wandered from God and was being oppressed by its enemies, the prophet Isaiah said:

> "Sing, O barren. You who have not borne! Break forth into singing, and cry aloud, you who have not laboured with child. For more are the children of the desolate than the married woman," says the Lord.

In the culture of Isaiah's day, barrenness was a terrible stigma. For a married woman, barrenness was her worst nightmare. Into that darkness, hopelessness and failure, God says, "Sing/praise—out loud!" Faith-filled praise from deep within the soul, brings the presence of God into the situation. This is what happened in 2 Chronicles 20 and in Acts 16. Psalm 22 verse three, in the King James version of the Bible, says, "Thou art holy, O thou that inhabits the praises of Israel."

This is what David discovered. As he hoped in God and praised Him, he felt the help of 'God's countenance'. In other words, he felt God's presence, as if God were looking upon him and saying to him, "I've got this David." But it does not stop there. As you read on, the New King James version as an interesting end to the psalm.

> Why are you cast down, O my soul? And why are you disquieted within me? Hope in God; for I will yet praise Him, the help of my countenance and my God. (Psalm 42:11)

This verse could be seen as a repeat of verse five but look at it again. In verse five, David, as he praises, feels the help of God's countenance. In verse eleven, as David continues praising, God's presence/God's countenance, causes David's countenance to change. Instead of looking miserable and downcast, David looks happy and joyful. David had discovered that remembering God's blessing in his life and praising God is the antidote to depression.

You might well be saying to yourself, "Easier said than done." True. But take it step by step. Firstly, recall God's blessings in your life, and if that is hard, recall some of the stories other people have shared of God's blessing and faithfulness. Put on your favourite praise music or praise on YouTube. At first, it may seem to be a struggle, but as you listen and then begin to join in, bit by bit, it will get easier, until you are able to praise from your heart!

Elijah

Our next 'virtual patient' is Elijah. I love Elijah. James describes him as a 'man with like passions as us' (James 5:17). He is introduced to us in 1 Kings seventeen as Elijah the Tishbite from Gilead. An ordinary kind of guy—not a priest, not royalty, not an aristocrat or anyone else thought to be important.

Elijah lived at a time when the nation Israel was wandering further and further away from God. The worship of Baal, the Canaanite fertility god, was on the increase and the worship of Jehovah, the true and living God, was on the decline. A decline not helped by the fact that Israel's king, Ahab, had married a controlling, Baal-worshipping queen, in the person of Jezebel. As the drumbeats sounded across the nation for people to go and worship Baal, as mothers sacrificed their babies in Baal worship fires, and as young women became Baal prostitutes, Elijah became increasingly burdened and disturbed.

I am sure Elijah thought to himself, "If no one else will do something about this, then I will." Elijah began to call upon God and search the Scriptures available to him. I am quite sure that it was not long before he came across the Scripture in Deuteronomy:

> Take heed to yourselves, lest your heart be deceived, and you turn aside and serve other gods and worship them, lest the Lord's anger be aroused against you, and He shut up the heavens so that there be no rain, and the land yield no produce, and you perish quickly from the good land which the Lord is giving you. (Deuteronomy 11:16-17)

That word burned into his heart. He began to pray over that word and cry out to God for the nation. Elijah, this ordinary man, becomes an intercessor. The word of God becomes so much part of him that he presents himself before Ahab, the king, and says:

> As the Lord God of Israel lives, before whom I stand, there shall not be dew no rain these years, except at my word.

Powerful. An ordinary man gets a word from God and prays it into being. What a challenge to us who live in a similar spiritual climate to that of Elijah.

From that first meeting with Ahab, Elijah is instructed to go to the brook Cherith. There he proves God for himself, as ravens bring him his daily food. When the brook Cherith dries up, Elijah is instructed to go to Zarephath. There he proves God to the ones and twos—to a widow and her son. They are about to eat their last meal.

Elijah instructs them to make him a meal first and then one for themselves. As the widow obeys his word, a miracle takes place, and they have food for the rest of the famine. From Zarephath, after three and a half years, it is time for

Elijah to prove God to the nation. A showdown is arranged between Elijah and the prophets and priests of Baal. The nation is summoned to watch. Each party is given a bull (which is cut in pieces), and the bull is laid on wood. The challenge:

> "Then you call on the name of your gods, and I will call on the name of the Lord; and the God who answers by fire, He is God." So, all the people answered and said, "It is well spoken." (1 Kings 18:24)

Elijah invites the Baal priests and prophets to go first. They start off confidently. In the occult practices of their religion, they were accustomed to conjuring up fire. That day, as hard as they tried, they could not even get a spark! One man of God, a man of prayer, a man with the word of God, in God's place at God's time, bound the powers of darkness! Then it's Elijah's turn. He calls the people to him.

He repairs the altar of the Lord and with twelve stones builds an altar in the name of the Lord and makes a trench around it. He puts the wood in order and then the bull pieces on top. He then asks the people to do something quite unusual. He asks them to get water (a scarce commodity in a time of drought) and poor it over the sacrifice—not just once but three times! It is surprising the lengths people will go to try and damp down the work of God. Then it is the time of the evening sacrifice, and Elijah prays:

> Lord God of Abraham, Isaac, and Israel, let it be known this day that You are God in Israel, and I am

your servant, and that I have done all these things at Your word. Hear me, O Lord, hear me, that this people may know that You are the Lord God, and that You have turned their hearts back to you again.

Then the fire of the Lord fell and consumed the sacrifice, and the wood and the stones and the dust and it licked up the water that was in the trench. (1 Kings 18:36-38)

When the people saw it, they fell on their faces and repeated, "The Lord, He is God!" Elijah commands the prophets of Baal to be seized and they are taken to the Brook Kishon and executed. What a day! But it is not over. Elijah goes back up Carmel, falls down with his face between his knees and starts praying for rain.

He sends his servant to look for a cloud. Nothing. Elijah, the seasoned intercessor, persists. On the seventh time, the servant reports a cloud the size of a man's hand. The rain is coming. Elijah outruns the king's chariot to Jezreel.

What a day! What an experience. Elijah must have felt the flush of success, satisfied that, at last, things were going to change in the nation. However, success is when we are most vulnerable. That is what we find with Elijah—the man with like passions as us.

Maybe Elijah felt that he would be called to the palace, be made prime minister, and become the chief spiritual director for the nation. What happened was the complete opposite. There was a message from the palace. A message from the irate, Baal-worshipping Jezebel, "So let the gods do to me, and more also, if I do not make your life as the life of one of the slain prophets of Baal by tomorrow about this time."

Elijah panics, and Elijah runs. His world has been turned upside down. Success has been turned on its head in a moment. Elijah is devastated. Instead of stopping and reflecting on all that God has done, he allows the demonised message of Jezebel to fill his mind. Not only does he run, but after a while he leaves his servant behind. Alone, exhausted, and isolated in a wilderness place, things can only get worse—and they do.

> But he himself went a day's journey into the wilderness and came and sat under a broom (juniper) tree. And he prayed that he might die, and he said, "It is enough! Now, Lord, take my life, for I am no better than my fathers!"

Elijah is exhausted, alone, confused, paranoid and suicidal. He feels like a failure. He's lost all sense of direction, motivation, and purpose. Elijah is depressed. So how does he escape this dark state of his soul? The next part of the Biblical narrative tells us.

> Then as he lay and slept under a broom tree, suddenly an angel touched him and said to him, "Arise and eat." Then he looked, and there by his head was a cake baked on the coals, and a jar of water. So, he ate and drank, and lay down again. And the angel of the Lord came back the second time, and said, "Arise and eat, because the journey is too great for you." So, he arose, and ate and drank and went in the strength of that food forty days and forty nights as far as Horeb, the mountain of God.

One response to Elijah feeling very sorry for himself and wanting to end it all could have been, "Pull yourself together, man. What's the matter with you? Forget your pity party." But not God. God's first response to this exhausted, depressed prophet, is fresh food, refreshing water and rest. As spiritual as Elijah might have appeared to be, as James reminds us, he is still a man with like passions as us.

Whilst his being involved in exciting spiritual encounters, such as was seen on Carmel, is amazing, he still needed to rest. So do we. The first step to overcoming depression may well be a restful holiday, beautiful scenery, and quality nourishing food.

I remember reading about the revival that occurred in recent times in Pensacola. The temptation for the leaders was to continue night after night without a break. But they had done their revival homework and recognised that they needed to have one day where there were no meetings so that their bodies could rest. The 1904 Welsh revival was amazing with thousands coming to Christ in a short period of time. However, the tragedy of that revival was that the principal revivalist, Evan Roberts, was left exhausted and experiencing a nervous breakdown. The Sabbath rest principle applies to everyone—even prophets and revivalists!

Well, Elijah arrives at Horeb, the mountain of God. There, he finds a cave and spends the night. God comes to him, and asks him, "What are you doing here?" Elijah replies with his well-rehearsed pity party speech.

> I have been very zealous for the Lord God of hosts; for the children of Israel have forgotten Your covenant, torn down Your altars, and have killed your

prophets with the sword. I alone am left; and they seek to take my life. (1 Kings 19:10)

Elijah is then told to go outside the cave and stand on the mountain before God. There is a strong wind tearing rocks into pieces, but God is not in the wind. Then, there is an earthquake, but God is not in the earthquake. This is followed by a fire, but God was not in the fire. Then a still small voice.

God is not in the spectacular but in the peace and the quiet. God again asks, "What are you doing here, Elijah?" Again, Elijah replies with his pity-part speech. Interestingly, God does not debate or argue with Elijah at this point. Instead of answering the 'why' question, God continues with the 'What next'.

God instructed Elijah to go and anoint Hazael as king over Syria, Jehu the son of Nimshi as king over Israel, and Elisha the son of Shaphat to be his successor. Only then does God say:

Yet I have reserved seven thousand in Israel, all whose knees have not bowed to Baal, and every mouth that has not kissed him. (1 Kings 19:18)

As we follow the Elijah story, we too can get exhausted, worn out and feel isolated and alone. We too can begin to think what is the point of it all. Like Elijah, we lose all sense of purpose and direction and enter a pity party dialogue of, "No one understands what I've done and what I'm going through." The antidote. As we have said, rest and relaxation and then hearing the still small voice of God, not answering our 'Whys' but telling us our 'What next'. In the words of Jeremiah:

> For I know the thoughts that I think toward you, says the Lord, thoughts of peace and not of evil, to give you a future and a hope. (Jeremiah 29:11)

What a joy it must have been for Elijah to train and mentor his successor, Elisha. A rejuvenated Elijah refocussed and discovered his 'What next'.

Paul

Adding the Apostle Paul's name to this virtual clinic might have come as a surprise to some. You would think that Paul was almost indestructible. He experienced being beaten, stoned, shipwrecked, and imprisoned—on more than one occasion, not to mention the perils of robbers, perils of his countrymen, perils of the Gentiles and often going hungry and thirsty. (2 Corinthians 11:22-28).

Paul had such a powerful call to ministry. Paul was the church planter, leadership developer and letter writer extraordinaire. Depressed? Unthinkable. Yet even this great Apostle suffered from this condition.

In 2 Corinthians, Paul writes:

> For indeed when we came to Macedonia, our bodies had no rest, but we were troubled on every side. Outside were conflicts, inside were fears. Nevertheless God, who comforts the downcast,

comforted us by the coming of Titus. (2 Corinthians 7:5-6)

There are some telling remarks in these verses. 'Our bodies had no rest'—he was not sleeping. 'Outside were conflicts'—real and imagined conflicts. 'Inside were fears' was quite a statement of how he was feeling, scared and unsure of himself, afraid of where the next attack was coming from. 'Who comforts the downcast'—he was experiencing a low mood. Paul had many of the characteristics of someone suffering from significant depression.

How did Paul become like this? As we go over the back story, it seemed to have occurred when Paul came to Macedonia. The call to go and preach the good news in Macedonia could not have been clearer. Acts sixteen tells us that Paul and his companions had tried to go to the Roman Province of Asia but had felt the Holy Spirit giving a strong 'no'.

They then tried to go to Bithynia but again, the Spirit did not permit them. It is then, in a vision, that Paul saw a man from Macedonia pleading for them to go there and help them. So, concluding that the Lord had called them there, off they went.

The mission starts pleasantly enough when they arrive at Philippi. A trader by the name of Lydia gets saved along with her household. They then meet a demonised slave girl, whose masters used her to make a profit for themselves through fortune-telling. She follows Paul and his party. She appears to be saying the right things when she says, "These are the servants of the Most High God, who proclaim to us the way of salvation."

The words may have been right, but the inspiration was all wrong. As the days passed, Paul became more and more annoyed by this girl's interruptions, until one day he turns to the girl, and speaking directly to the evil spirit, a spirit of divination, says, "I command you in the name of Jesus Christ to come out of her."

The demon left that very hour. That was good for Paul and his party and good for the girl, but it was not good as far as her masters were concerned. The girl was no longer useful for fortune-telling. Her masters cause an uproar in the city and Paul and Silas are brought before the magistrates. They are flogged and thrown into the innermost prison.

Locked in stocks, their backs sore and their limbs aching, Paul and Silas decide to praise God. At midnight, they start singing and the prisoners heard them! What a response! But their response is heard in heaven. God always takes note when his people begin praising. In fact, He more than takes note when that praise is an act of faith in a difficult situation.

Suddenly, there is an earthquake. The prison is shaken, all the doors are opened, and everyone's chains are loosed (not only are those praising the beneficiaries of their praise but everyone else around them!). The jailer, thinking everyone has escaped is about to kill himself—rather than face a Roman tribunal and be executed anyway.

Paul calls out to him. "Do yourself no harm, for we are all here." The next moment the jailer falls down before Paul and Silas and asks, "What must I do to be saved?" Paul answers in beautiful Gospel words:

> Believe on the Lord Jesus Christ, and you will be saved, you and your household. (Acts 16:31)

The whole household gathers to hear the word of God. Paul and Silas have their wounds treated and then conduct a baptismal service for the jailer and his household. After the baptisms, they all enjoy a meal together. The next day, the magistrates instruct them to be released.

It is then that Paul tells them that they had Roman citizenship and that it was wrong that they had been beaten without a proper trial. The magistrates are made to eat humble pie. They ask Paul and Silas to leave the city.

From Philippi, they travel to Thessalonica. Paul, as was his custom, goes to the synagogue and starts sharing the Gospel, and over three weeks a number become believers. However, some of the Jews were not at all happy and create an uproar in the city, saying that Paul was undermining the authority of Caesar by proclaiming that there is another king—Jesus. Paul was not present when the uproar took place and the believers send Paul and Silas away, for their own protection, by night to Berea.

At Berea, they once again go into the synagogue and share the Good News of Jesus. There is a good response. However, the Jews at Thessalonica hear about it and come to Berea and stir up the crowds. Paul, being the main speaker, again, for his own safety, is sent away to Athens.

Paul is now on his own. Trouble is following him wherever he goes. Hardly does he begin in a place, and then he has to leave. This was all beginning to get to him. At Athens, he sees idolatry on every corner, and he cannot keep quiet.

He starts reasoning with the people. Some philosophers start debating with him and Paul is invited to speak at the Areopagus on Mars Hill. He struggles to get his message across. Some believed but the majority mocked him or were dismissive of his message. From Athens, Paul makes his way to Corinth.

All that had happened in just a few weeks, gets to him. The repeated trouble, resistance to the message, threats, and mocking crowds had taken their toll on Paul's mental health.

> For indeed when we came to Macedonia, our bodies had no rest, but we were troubled on every side. Outside were conflicts, inside were fears. Nevertheless God, who comforts the downcast, comforted us by the coming of Titus. (2 Corinthians 7:5-6)

Paul was depressed. But how did he overcome this depression? Like many Jews with his education, Paul had a trade. Paul's trade was that of a tentmaker. When he arrived in Corinth, Paul finds Aquila and Priscilla, a Jewish Christian couple, who were also tentmakers. Paul is able to start working with them (Acts 18:3).

Here, we discover the first steps in Paul's rehabilitation. Meeting other people, chatting, and taking time out and doing something useful and creative with his hands. We saw it with Elijah, rest and recreation are vital to our well-being. For some, it may be music, others art, others making things or playing golf and so the list goes on.

Depression wants to keep you looking inward and alone. Breaking its grip involves meeting other people and beginning to talk, and even better, if you can do some activity together.

Step two for Paul's overcoming depression was the coming of Titus. Part of Paul's problem had been to start doubting whether what he had gone through had been worthwhile. Depression has a way of doing that to us. However, Titus shows up and then Silas and Timothy. Titus is able to share how well the newly founded churches in Philippi and Thessalonica are doing.

How the new Christians are rejoicing in the Lord and bravely sharing their faith. In fact, in Thessalonica, an evangelistic revival was taking place (1 Thessalonians 1:8). Paul was encouraged by the reports and words of his friends. Encouraging words are powerful! Even framing our words in a positive manner makes a difference.

Instead of the glass being half empty, it is half full! This is a principle made use of in cognitive behavioural therapy (CBT). Long before CBT, the Bible speaks of us, "Being transformed by the renewing of our minds" (Romans 12:2).

Step three in overcoming depression was the power of the team. Paul may have been a well-educated and gifted man, but on his own, he was vulnerable. With a team around him, supporting, encouraging, and praying for him, he was stronger. Sharing ideas, iron sharpening iron, and together praying issues through, made for a better Paul.

> When Silas and Timothy had come from Macedonia, Paul was compelled by the Spirit, and testified to the Jews that Jesus is the Christ. (Acts 18:5)

An important partner in the work of God is the Holy Spirit. Without Him, we can do nothing. With the encouragement of his team, Paul once again tunes into the power and person of the Holy Spirit—who Himself is the great comforter and counsellor.

Step four, for Paul to overcome depression, was to get a clear word from the Lord Himself.

> Now the Lord spoke to Paul in the night by a vision, Do not be afraid, but speak, and do not keep silent; for I am with you, and no one will attack you to hurt you; for I have many people in this city.

No attacks, no physical harm, and the promise of a fruitful ministry. What a word! God is the ultimate comforter. No wonder Paul begins his second letter to the Corinthians with the words:

> Blessed be the God and Father of our Lord Jesus Christ, the Father of mercies and God of all comfort, who comforts us in all our tribulations, that we may be able to comfort those who are in any trouble, with the comfort with which we are comforted by God. (2 Corinthians 1:3-4)

With such a word, Paul is able to embark on eighteen months of productive ministry at Corinth. We saw with Elijah, getting the 'What next' word is so important. Here we see something of the same with Paul. The route out of depression included rest, recreation, companionship, encouragement, and renewed direction for the future. That route has not changed!

Chapter 8
RIP Anxiety

It is the night before an important examination. You are about to perform in front of a large group of people. You have an interview for a job you desperately want. How do you feel? On edge, nervous and anxious are some of the words that come to mind.

Your heart is racing a little, you have butterflies in your stomach, your hands are clammy, and your mouth is dry. These are some of the physical symptoms you may have. Should we be experiencing these things? Yes. They are part of a normal physiological response, commonly known as the 'flight or fight' response.

When faced with a potentially dangerous or frightening situation, our bodies have this in-built mechanism whereby adrenaline is released, our heart rate and breathing rate speed up, our blood pressure goes up, our muscles tense, our pupils dilate, our thinking speeds up and we are ready to run! And if we cannot run, then we fight! The diversion of blood from the stomach and periphery to the major muscles is why we get the 'butterfly stomach' and cold clammy hands. Another downside is that the bladder muscles may relax resulting in an unfortunate accident—wetting ourselves.

When facing that exam, performance or interview, a measure (not an overload) of the 'flight or fight' response will actually be beneficial. Your thought processing will be sharpened, and your performance enhanced. So this physiological response can be helpful to us, and in a truly dangerous or frightening situation, may well be lifesaving. However, if this response begins to kick in inappropriately, then we have a problem. If non-threatening things are perceived as threatening or if our mind races with anxious thoughts and sets off the 'flight or fright' response, then we are going to need to get it under control.

If not, then we are going to get breathless and tight-chested, have palpitations and tremble and because we are not actually fleeing or fighting, we are likely to become light-headed and even faint. A look online will give you a list of breathing exercises (e.g. taking in a slow deep breath and then slowly breathing out, counting up to ten), relaxation techniques and other psychological interventions that can be tried to control an inappropriate 'flight or fight' response. We saw that with depression there is an assessment tool called PHQ-9. Similarly, with anxiety, there is an assessment tool called GAD-7[17].

As with depression, cognitive behavioural therapy (CBT) and counselling will also have a large part to play in treating and managing anxiety. In this chapter, we ask the question, "What does the Bible say about anxiety and irrational fear?" We live in a world where there appears to be an epidemic of anxiety, not helped by the Covid pandemic, the cost-of-living

---

[17] Devon Partnership NHS Trust www.dpt.nhs.uk Appendix B: PHQ-9-7 GAD.

crisis, economic uncertainty, political instability, and wars and rumours of war. Thankfully, we can find answers in the teachings of Jesus.

In the sermon, called the Sermon on the Mount, covering three chapters in the Gospel of Matthew, Jesus dedicates a whole section to the subject of anxiety (Matthew 6:25-34). He begins with the words:

> Therefore, I say to you, do not worry about your life, what you will eat or drink; nor about your body, what you will put on. Is not life more than food and the body more than clothing? (Matthew 6:25)

He continues:

> Therefore, do not worry, saying, 'What shall we eat?' or 'What shall we drink?' or 'What shall we wear?' For after all these things the Gentiles seek. For your heavenly Father knows that you have need of these things. But seek first the kingdom of God and His righteousness and all these things shall be added to you. Therefore, do not worry about tomorrow, for tomorrow will worry about its own things. Sufficient for the day is its own trouble. (Matthew 6:31-34)

God our Father

Jesus's first antidote to worry is this, God is our Father. The phrase 'heavenly Father' could make God seem distant, but He is not. Scripture shows us that He is Abba Father.

'Abba' is the Aramaic equivalent of 'Dad' or 'Daddy'. It speaks of a close relationship.

Jesus, when praying to His Father, used the word 'Abba'. During a time of intense anguish, praying in Gethsemane, Jesus prays, "Abba, Father, all things are possible for You. Take this cup away from Me; nevertheless, not what I will, but what you will" (Mark 14:36). When we become born-again Christian believers, the New Testament tells us that we receive the Spirit of adoption, whereby we can call out 'Abba, Father'.

> For you did not receive the spirit of bondage again to fear, but you received the Spirit of adoption by whom we cry out, "Abba, Father." The Spirit Himself bears witness with our spirit that we are the children of God. (Romans 8:15-16)
> And because you are sons, God has sent forth the Spirit of His Son into your hearts, crying out, "Abba, Father!" (Galatians 4:6)

Thank God, we are not just forgiven sinners. We have not just been declared righteous and set apart for God. No more! We, by grace, are children of the living God, the Creator of the Universe and we can call Him, "Abba, Father!" How good is that!

God is love. It goes without saying that as a Father, He is a loving Father.

> Behold what manner love the Father has bestowed on us, that we should be called children of God! (1 John 3:1)

His love is best described in the Greek word, 'Agape'. This is the love whereby someone is prepared to sacrifice him/herself for another. It is a love that loves the unlovely. It is a love that is consistent and true. It is a love that knows no end. It is because of this love, Jesus died in our place upon the cross. This is the love Paul so eloquently writes about in 1 Corinthians 13:

> Love suffers long and is kind; love does not envy; love does not parade itself, is not puffed up; does not behave rudely, does not seek its own, is not provoked, thinks no evil; does not rejoice in iniquity, but rejoices in the truth; bears all things, believes all things, endures all things. Love never fails. (1 Corinthians 13:4-8)

To be loved like this is amazing. Meditating upon this love, reflecting on this love, and resting in this love, is truly an antidote to worry and anxiety. Remember, Romans chapter 8 says, "Nothing can separate us from this love" (Romans 8:38-39).

But not only is God a loving Father, He is a wise Father. He knows what is best for us. As earthly parents, there are times when we have had to hold back on giving our children what they have wanted, because either, it was inappropriate, they were not mature enough to manage it or because we knew there was something better for them. If that is the case with earthly parents, then how much more our heavenly Father, the fountain of all wisdom?

Not only is He loving and wise, but He is also the eternal Father, our Father who is in heaven. As such, He can see the end from the beginning. He is above time and the past, the present and the future are all one to Him. He is the eternal 'I am'. This may sound deep, but when we cast our worries and cares upon Him, He says, "I've got it."

> Jesus said, "Come unto Me, all you who labour and are heavy laden, and I will give you rest. Take My yoke upon you and learn from Me, for I am gentle and lowly in heart, and you will find rest for your souls. For my yoke is easy and my burden is light." (Matthew 11:28-29)
>
> Casting all your care upon Him, for He cares for you. (1 Peter 5:7)

In life, it can seem there are times we are walking in the midst of skyscrapers. Everything is overwhelming and intimidating. Coming to our heavenly Father is like jumping in an aeroplane and flying high above those same skyscrapers. Not only do they now seem like matchboxes, but we can see beyond them to the beautiful countryside and open space.

When Jesus was teaching on prayer, He said that we should begin praying by saying, "Our Father." If He had only given us those two words, then that would have been enough to revolutionise our prayer life. Yes, God is our heavenly Father. He is loving, He is wise, and He is eternal. If we can fix our minds upon these powerful thoughts, and daily renew our minds in this way, spending time in prayer, focussing on the Father, then we are going to go a long way to overcoming our fears, worries and anxieties.

God our Master

In this passage in the Sermon on the Mount. Jesus not only says that God is our Father, but that He is our Lord and Master.

> No one can serve two masters; for either he will hate the one and love the other, or else he will be loyal to one and despise the other. You cannot serve God and mammon. (Matthew 6:24)
> But seek first the kingdom of God and His righteousness and all these things shall be added to you. Therefore, do not worry about tomorrow, for tomorrow will worry about its own things. Sufficient for the day is its own trouble. (Matthew 6:33)

In the west, we tend to be very possessive of all that we have. My life, my job, my home, my time, my money... and so the list goes on. When we accept Jesus as our Saviour and Lord, that all changes (or it should do!). In his letter to the Corinthians, Paul writes:

> For you are bought at a price; therefore, glorify God in your body and in your spirit, which are God's. (1 Corinthians 6:20)

All that we have, all that we are, and all that we ever hope to be, is His! In the final verse of the Isaac Watts hymn, "When I survey, the wondrous Cross," Watts writes, "Love so amazing, so Divine, demands my life, my soul, my all." Jesus is teaching this in such parables as the 'Parable of the pearl of great price' (Matthew 13:45-46).

When both John the Baptist and Jesus began their ministries, they preached, "Repent, for the kingdom of God is at hand." Literally, turn from the way you are going, and experience the liberating rule of God. The kingdom of God (as we touched on in an earlier chapter) is literally the rule of God. In the past, it was manifest in God's rule in the nation of Israel. In the future, it will be manifest when Christ comes again and reigns and rules. But right now, the kingdom of God is the rule of God, by the Spirit of God in the lives of believers.

> For the kingdom of God is not eating and drinking, but righteousness and peace and joy in the Holy Spirit. (Romans 14:17)

Jesus, in the Sermon on the Mount, is saying that as we 'seek first this kingdom'—the kingdom of God—the rule of God by the Spirit of God, then everything else will be added to us. When we truly surrender every part of our lives to Him, then He becomes the Master and we become the manager. That means we no longer have to worry about things! We just tell the Master. The wonderful thing is that God is such a good Master that as we yield and surrender our lives, our all to Him, He abundantly blesses us in return!

Peter

Does it work? Well, consider Simon Peter. During Jesus' three-year ministry, Peter had a reputation for being the guy who opened his mouth and put his foot in it! At the Last Supper, Jesus told the disciples that they would all stumble and be scattered.

Peter answers, "Even if all are made to stumble because of You, I will never be made to stumble."

Jesus said to him, "Assuredly, I say to you that this night, before the rooster crows, you will deny me three times" (Matthew 26:33-34).

Peter was to eat his own words. At Jesus's trial (and things are not going well for Jesus), when approached by a servant girl who said that he had been with Jesus, Peter vehemently denies it. Then another servant girl says much the same thing. Again, Peter denies it. Then a group of people comment on his speech and that he must be one of Jesus' disciples.

Again, but this time with cursing and swearing, he makes a firm denial. The cock crows. (Matthew 26:69-75), Peter was too afraid to confess Jesus before a servant girl. Fear and anxiety got the better of him. He felt it was the end—but it was not.

I love Mark's account of the resurrection of Jesus. The angel says to the three women who were first to visit the tomb, "Do not be alarmed. You seek Jesus of Nazareth who was crucified. He is risen! He is not here. See the place where they laid Him. But go and tell His disciples——and Peter——that He is going before you into Galilee; therefore, you shall see Him, as He said to you" (Mark 16: 6-7).

Note that a special mention of Peter. The Great Shepherd has one of His sheep particularly mentioned. That must have been such an encouragement to Peter, but it does not end there. John's Gospel, chapter 21, tells us what happened at Galilee. Peter and the other disciples go fishing.

Pause there a moment. I have heard preachers say that they were backsliding by returning to their old habits and trade. I want to scream out, "Wrong!" After the trauma and turmoil of what had happened in Jerusalem, the baying crowds, the flogging and crucifixion of Jesus, and the uncertainty of what might happen to them—I believe Jesus intended for His disciples to get out of the city and get some rest and recreation. We saw in the earlier chapter that's exactly what Elijah and Paul needed, and if you have been through a traumatic and tough time, you more than likely need it as well!

The story continues. The disciples spend all night fishing but do not catch a thing. The next morning, as the sun rises and the sea mists clear, they see a fire on the shore, and they smell freshly cooked bread and fish. A voice calls out, "Children have you any food?"

They reply, "No."

Jesus says, "Cast the net on the right side of the boat, and you will find some."

They did, and they caught a whole pile of fish. (John 21:5-6). John, then Peter, recognised it is the Lord. Way back at the beginning of Jesus ministry, the same miraculous catch took place, when Jesus called Peter and Andrew, James, and John, to be his disciples.

Peter, being Peter, plunges into the sea and swims ashore, such was his excitement at being able to see Jesus again. The other disciples join them, having pulled the catch of fish ashore. Together they all have breakfast.

It is only after breakfast that Jesus takes Peter aside. Note that—warmed, refreshed, and fed (again, compare with Elijah). Three times Jesus asks Peter, "Do you love Me?" Interesting. There had been three denials by Peter. By the third time, Peter is getting upset. Peter's reply is, "Lord you know all things; You know that I love You." Then we come to a significant statement.

> Jesus said to him. "Feed my sheep. Most assuredly, I say to you, when you were younger, you girded yourself and walked where you wished; but when you are old, you will stretch out your hands, and another will gird you and carry you where you do not wish." This He spoke, signifying by what death he would glorify God. And when He had spoken this, He said to Him, "Follow Me."

Not a pleasant word, but from that moment on Peter's fears and anxieties were laid to rest. Jesus was risen from the dead. Jesus's words were 100% dependable. Peter knew that from that day on, he would live for Jesus and die for Jesus. Jesus was His Lord and Master.

Fast forward to Acts chapter twelve. The wicked King Herod decides to harass the church. He has James, the brother of John, killed with the sword. Because this action pleased the religious Jews, Herod has Peter arrested, with the intention of having Peter brought before the people and executed after the Passover Feast. Four squads of four soldiers to each squad were assigned to guard Peter.

Added to that, Peter was fastened by two chains between two soldiers, and guards were watching the prison door. Talk about tight security! Meanwhile, the church was praying constantly, day and night, for Peter. Here is the question. If you were Peter, given the uncomfortable surroundings, rough guards on either side of you, heavy chains binding you, and knowing it is the eve of your execution, what would you be doing? The Peter we saw at the trial of Jesus would have been beside himself with fear and anxiety. But not now. Peter was sound asleep! In fact, he was sleeping so deeply that an angel had to shake him, to wake him up.

> Now behold, an angel of the Lord stood by him, and a light shone in the prison; and he struck Peter on the side and raised him up, saying, "Arise quickly!" And his chains fell off his hands. Then the angel said to him, "Gird yourself and tie on your sandals;" and so, he did. And he said to him, "Put on your garment and follow me."
> So, he went out and followed him, and did not know that what was done by the angel was real, but thought he was seeing a vision. When they were past the first and second guard posts, they came to the iron gate that leads to the city, which opened to them of its own accord; and they went out and went down one street, and immediately the angel departed from him.
> And when Peter had come to himself, he said, "Now I know for certain that the Lord has sent His angel and has delivered me from the hand of Herod and from all the expectation of the Jewish people." (Acts 12:7-12)

What a story! A story with an amusing ending. It was easier for Peter to get out of prison than to get into the prayer meeting! On release, Peter goes to the home of Mary, the mother of John Mark, where believers pray through the night. A young girl answers the door but, in her excitement at seeing Peter, leaves him on the doorstep!

I can imagine her going and whispering to one of the leaders of the meeting that Peter was at the door. She was rebuked! "You are imagining things. It is his angel!" But she persisted, as did Peter, knocking on the door. Eventually, the door opened, and they were all astonished (Acts 12:12-17).

The words of Paul

Paul had experienced enough in his own life to know that being a Christian leader in the first century was no easy thing. He writes to one of his prodigies, Timothy:

> For God has not given us a spirit of fear, but of power and of love and of a sound mind. (2 Timothy 1:7)

Here, Paul gives Timothy, and us, three antidotes to fear and anxiety. The first one is the abiding presence, person, and power of the Holy Spirit. In John's Gospel, Jesus repeatedly talks about the Holy Spirit (John 14:16-18, 26; John 15:26-27; John 16:7-15). Depending on which Bible version you are using, the Holy Spirit is described as being the Helper, the Comforter, or the Counsellor. In fact, He is all three and more! In Greek, He is the 'paraclete'—the one who comes alongside us.

In fact, if we did not know any Greek, it is clear in the words of Jesus, "I will not leave you as orphans; I will come to you" (John 14:18). Having the Holy Spirit in us and with us, is just like having Jesus. How important it is then to be filled, and keep on being filled, with the Holy Spirit. Hungering and thirsting for Him, opening our hearts and lives up to Him, in prayer, praise and worship.

I have known times in my life when I have begun to get anxious about something. My mind has been racing trying to think through what could happen. But then, I have spent time in God's presence, either alone or with God's people, praising and exalting the Lord Jesus Christ, and the anxious thoughts have disappeared, replaced by a deep peace that God is in control.

The second antidote to fear and anxiety that Paul gives is love. Not just any kind of love but God's love. We have already shared about the Father's love in this chapter. How important it is to meditate upon His love, rest in His love, confess His love and feel secure in His love.

The third antidote is that God gives us a sound mind. In the second half of 1 Corinthians 2:16, it says, "But we have the mind of Christ." For a moment think of some of the things Jesus did. For example, Jesus spent much time in communion with the Father. He lived His life in the Father's will. He came not to be served but to serve. When He saw the hurting and broken, He was moved with compassion. Philippians chapter two says:

> Let this mind be in you, which was also in Christ Jesus, who being in the form of God, did not consider it robbery to be equal with God, but made Himself of no reputation, taking the form of a bondservant, and coming in the likeness of man. And being found in appearance as a man, He humbled Himself and became obedient to the point of death, even the death of the cross. Therefore, God has highly exalted Him and given Him the name which is above every other name, that bat the name of Jesus every knee should

bow, of those in heaven, and of those on earth, and of those under the earth, and that every tongue should confess that Jesus Christ is Lord, to the glory of God the Father. (Philippians 2:5-11)

If we begin, through prayer, to align our minds with the mind of Jesus, then we too can begin to know the peace of Jesus.

> Be anxious for nothing, but in everything by prayer and supplication, with thanksgiving, let your requests be made known to God; and the peace of God, which surpasses all understanding, will guard your hearts and minds through Christ Jesus. (Philippians 4:6-7)

Let us apply spiritual CBT (cognitive behavioural therapy) and be transformed by the renewing of our minds! (Romans 12:2).

Chapter 9
Loss

She was our first child. A beautiful baby girl, named Sarah—our little princess. Like any new parents, there was the joy of phoning and telling our own parents that they were now grandparents, and soon the news spread. Everyone rejoiced with us in the safe arrival of our baby girl. The congratulatory cards began to arrive, and for three and a half weeks, we experienced joy, mixed with disturbed sleep, as we took our first steps as new parents.

Then one night, she did not wake for her four hourly feeds. My wife felt concerned, and so I, sleepily, began to check Sarah over. She seemed more floppy than usual, and her colour was not right. I checked her temperature. It was just over 38 degrees Celsius.

Something was not right. I called the on-call GP. He was not at all helpful. "Bring her to the surgery in the morning," was his advice. I had only been a doctor for less than two years, but even I knew that a neonate with an elevated temperature needed urgent attention. Add to that, a mother's intuition. It did not take us long to realise that we needed to rush our little baby to the hospital.

At the hospital, the paediatric doctors quickly got to work on Sarah. Despite it being the early hours of the morning, they were able to make a diagnosis of meningitis. Later, laboratory tests would show that it was a pneumococcal form of meningitis. Sarah was getting worse. Whilst the doctors and nurses were preparing to intubate and ventilate her, we phoned a pastor we knew well.

Despite it being extremely early in the morning, he answered his phone. "Pastor, our little baby girl is extremely sick. They are not sure if she will make it. Can you come and pray with us, for a miracle." Before the phone call ended, a doctor came into the room and said, "I am sorry. Your baby has had a respiratory and cardiac arrest. She is gone." Shocked and numbed, at just 24 years old, we were experiencing grief.

Grief process

Grief has been described as coming in five stages.[18] Originally described in patients with terminal illnesses and facing their own deaths, it has come to be recognised as a process experienced by everyone going through grief. Five stages may make it sound as though there is some set pattern to go through. The truth is grief is not linear, and different people will process it in different ways. Add to that, different cultures and different religious experiences (or none) and grief is going to manifest in different ways to different people.

Even with five stages, some people will get stuck at various stages, whilst others may miss a stage altogether. Complicated grief, where there has been an unexpected death

---

[18] Elizabeth Kubler-Ross, Death and Dying, 1969.

or a violent death (such as a traffic accident, murder, or suicide) is going to result in a more severe grief reaction, particularly in the initial stages. With these variations in mind, let us take a look at the five stages.

Stage 1: Denial. Some might add a stage before this one. The stage of shock. Whether you want to make shock a separate stage or not, shock, numbness and denial can be grouped together as part of stage one. Phrases such as, 'I think you've got this wrong, they'll be back soon', 'Impossible. They keep fit and well', 'It is not their time yet. They were given another six months' or 'I cannot believe it. It is unreal. It is a nightmare dream. I will wake up in a moment', may be spoken at this stage.

Alongside words (or no words) there will be a range of emotional outbursts including inconsolable crying and sobbing. Moving on from this stage will include repeating the story to visitors or on the telephone, seeing the deceased and going to the funeral. The key role of visitors is to be supportive and listen. In the Bible, even Job's friends, who became unhelpful, started off well, in this regard.

> Now when Job's three friends heard of all this adversity (Job had lost his herds and flocks and his eight children had all been killed in a freak windstorm) that had come upon him, each one came from his own place—Eliphaz the Temanite, Bildad the Shuhite and Zophar the Naamathite. For they had made an appointment together to come and comfort him, and to mourn for him.
> And when they raised their eyes from afar, and did not recognise him, they lifted their voices and wept;

> and each one tore his robe and sprinkled dust on his head toward heaven. So, they sat down with him on the ground seven days and seven nights, and no one spoke a word to him, for they saw that his grief was very great. (Job 1:11-13)

At this stage (and possibly in subsequent stages), it is not unusual, in a close relationship, for the bereaved person to think they have seen the deceased, heard their voice or felt their presence. This is not abnormal. A phrase sometimes used for people who have had a close relationship is that they are soul mates. The mind, emotions, and all that make up the soul can take time to catch up with the physical reality that the loved one has now passed away.

Stage 2: Anger. 'This is so unfair. This is so cruel', 'We should have gone to the doctor sooner', 'How did we miss this?' Anger against God is not unusual. 'God why did you allow this to happen?' Even anger at the deceased. 'Why did you go and die, now? We had so much to do, together'. Being free to express how you feel is an important part of processing this stage. One of the comforting aspects of the book of Psalms is to read how the Psalmist feels free to express his feelings. Needless to say, he does not stay there, but it is an important part of processing what he is going through.

> My God, my God, why have you forsaken me? Why are you so far from helping me, and from the words of my groaning? O my God, I cry in the daytime, but you do not hear; and in the night season and am not silent. (Psalm 22:1-2—prophetic words that Jesus Himself spoke from the Cross)

Again, like stage one, in supporting the bereaved, it is important to just listen and just be there, not to argue and debate.

Stage 3: Bargaining. This stage includes the 'What ifs', 'Could we have done things differently?' 'Why God? Why now?' We find a lot of this stage in Job's replies to his 'friends'.

> Even today my complaint is bitter; my hand is listless because of my groaning. Oh, that I knew where I might find Him (God), that I might come to His seat! I would present my case before Him and fill my mouth with arguments. (Job 23:1-4)

Our response to the bereaved is much the same as stage two. Certainly not the condemnatory words of Job's so-called friends! There will be a time when the 'Why?' can be replaced by the 'What next?' but that is at a later stage in the grief process.

Stage 4: Depression. This tends to be the longest and most difficult stage. Low mood, tearfulness, fragile emotions, lack of concentration, lack of motivation, lack of personal care, disturbed appetite, disturbed sleep and not socially mixing, can be some of the features of this stage. What can contribute to this phase is the sudden dropping of visitors. After the initial bereavement and up until the funeral, there are often visitors in abundance and family members giving support.

After the funeral, generally speaking, the visitors are not so frequent and family members have to get back to their regular routines. To help get through this stage involves people coming alongside. Things such as rides out into the countryside or by the sea, hairdressing appointments, bit by bit meeting other people, exercising, talking about the deceased and reliving memories are the kind of things that help, alongside re-engaging in spiritual activities such as prayer, worship, and Bible reading. Being with others who have gone through or are going through a similar experience can be helpful (can be, because different people experience grief in different ways). Organisations like CRUSE—Bereavement Support—are extremely helpful in helping deal with grief and can be contacted online.[19]

Stage 5: Acceptance. This is a gradual phase. Much depends on the closeness of the relationship with the deceased, how big the circle of friends is and whether the bereaved person is in employment. Certainly, this is the stage where the 'Why?' should now be replaced with the 'What next' questions. Engaging in new activities, meeting new people and travelling are a few of the things that occur at this stage.

How long does grief last? The answer to that question is going to vary from person to person, and the depth of the relationship, but a rough guide time is six to twelve months. That said, birthdays and anniversaries are going to be times when the bereaved person is likely to revisit their grief. Emotions are only just below the surface and any event that brings back a memory of a loved one may cause those emotions to surface.

---

[19] Cruse bereavement support—online—cruse.org.uk.

Our story

It would be an understatement to say that we were devastated when our three-and-a-half-week-old baby died. For days, it seemed like the world stopped. It all seemed unreal. I recall being handed a newspaper. On the front cover was a picture of someone called 'Red Robbo' in a celebratory pose because he had been one of the prime instigators in causing a strike at a large car manufacturing plant.

I threw the paper down in disgust. "Sir, there are more important things in life than your strike," I thought to myself. Going over the story of what had happened—or trying to between tears, was part of the process of getting over this stage. Just people being with us, saying little, was so helpful and supportive. It was good to feel that we were not on our own.

From a wider circle of people, sympathy cards and letters began to arrive. These were helpful—although one letter was written in the style of Job's friends and challenged us to examine our hearts, as we must have sinned! Thankfully, we have strong Christian faith, in a God who is the God of all comfort, the God of mercy and grace.

The funeral day came. There had been a heavy fall of snow, causing some disruption, but thankfully, everything could go ahead as planned. We felt ushered along. It was difficult to focus. The pastor, whom we had phoned in the middle of the night, took the service.

It was a simple service, but one filled with the hope we have in Jesus that one day we shall meet again. Travelling to the cemetery, the little white-clad coffin was on the front seat of the funeral car. Everything within me wanted there to be a resurrection miracle, then and there, but it was not to be.

Because of the weather conditions, the graveside service was short, and we were soon ushered back into the car and returned to our home.

In the days and weeks afterwards, I had to return to work. I was doing a training job in General Practice as well as pastoring the church in Pontllanfraith. The church was really supportive and although the number of visitors dropped, those who did visit knew what it was just to be there, to be a support and comfort, but not say too much. Important for both of us, but particularly for my wife.

Our Christian faith remained strong. If anything, it was stronger, but still, there was that deep longing to know the bigger picture, 'Why us?' 'Why now?' My wife's biggest concern was that life would go on and she would forget Sarah. For me, it was a month or so later that God spoke to me through the Scriptures (this is the way that God most often speaks). It was one of those 'rama' words.

> A little one shall become a thousand, and a small one a strong nation. I the Lord will hasten it in its time. (Isaiah 60:22)

I still did not understand everything, but now I had a 'word'. That word became my focus. In fact, the church began to grow. We were able to embark on a building programme and put up a two-hundred-seater new church building. That in itself was an incredible faith journey.

The sacrificial giving was amazing. Once we were in the new building, we saw further growth. At one point, baptismal services were taking place every month. It seemed the 'word' was coming to pass. One day, I prayed, "Lord, I can see that a thousand is possible, but what about the nation?" God is no man's debtor! Within a week of praying that prayer, I was contacted by the BBC, asking me if I would take part in the televised programme, 'Songs of Praise'.

This programme was going to be broadcast from a chapel in Crosskeys. My contribution would be to choose a hymn and then be interviewed about it, and then the hymn would be sung in the packed church, along with others. I chose the hymn, "My Jesus, I love thee, I know thou art mine." It was an opportunity to share my faith. The interviewer and I got along well, and so when I was speaking to the camera, I was not too nervous. The programme was broadcast to the whole nation, not just once but twice (repeat in mid-week).

It was then broadcast again, just to the nation of Wales. The BBC received several letters regarding my contribution to the broadcast. In one letter, a lady from Hastings wrote, "Thank you for last Sunday's 'Songs of Praise'. I was so moved by what the young doctor said that I got down on my knees, and said, 'God, please give me what the doctor has!'" I am quite sure the Lord knew exactly what she meant!

My wife continued to feel a sense of loss and sadness for many months. One Sunday, she paid a visit to her home church. After the service she found herself talking to two older ladies who had known her from her childhood days. She shared with them about the loss and how she did not want to forget Sarah. They prayed with her. They asked God to heal her of a broken heart and to show Sharon that she would not forget Sarah.

About a week later, Sharon was in the kitchen, when she felt God speaking to her, asking her to get down on her knees. She did what the Lord asked, and then she found herself being given a vision. In the vision, it was as if the Lord was taking her up a high mountain. At the top, He asked her, "What do you see?"

She replied, "Lord there is a beautiful view, but there is a problem. There is a big boulder blocking the view."

The Lord replied, "I know. That boulder represents your baby, Sarah Louise. Now, I want you to push that boulder."

In the vision, Sharon tried, but in her own strength could not. She said, "Lord, I cannot push this boulder. It is too big for me."

The Lord said, "I will help you."

Then, with the Lord's help, they together pushed the boulder, and the boulder began to roll down the mountainside. The boulder kept rolling and rolling. The Lord then said, "Now what do you see?"

Sharon replied, "I see a beautiful view and I can see the boulder rolling and rolling."

The Lord responded, "That boulder will always be there rolling and rolling in the distance. Your baby will not be forgotten. The view represents the future I have for you."

That vision was a huge turning point for Sharon. Two years after the loss of Sarah, we had our second child. A baby boy. Each year we visit Sarah's grave on, or as near as possible to, her birthday. We lay flowers, we shed tears and we pray. The boulder is still rolling!

Other forms of loss

The grief reaction not only occurs following the death of a loved one but also occurs in other forms of loss. When

Elizabeth Kubler-Ross[20] first described the stages of grief, it was in relationship to patients who had a terminal illness and were facing their own deaths. The same could apply to illnesses, other than terminal illness, where a patient has been told that they have an illness that is going to be life-changing or an accident that results in life-changing injuries. Then there is the loss of a job or the failure of an important examination. The breakdown of a marriage, particularly where one partner was not expecting it, can precipitate a strong grief reaction.

In many ways, this can be harder than experiencing the loss of a loved one through death. Anger, resentment, guilt and loss of self-worth are going to be to the fore—yet, all the time, knowing the former partner is still alive. Then there is the legal process and court appearances. A lot of support will be needed, but finding security in God's love and knowing that He has a plan and purpose for their life, will be key in coming through this particularly cruel form of grief. No wonder, Malachi, the prophet, says:

> The Lord has been witness between you and the wife of your youth, with whom you have dealt treacherously…
> For the Lord God of Israel says that He hates divorce. For it covers one's garment with violence. (Malachi 2:14, 16)

---

[20] Elizabeth Kubler-Ross, Death and Dying, 1969.

Suicide

Any form of violent death is going to be difficult to come to terms with. Added to the stages of grief will be an inquest and in the case of homicide, a trial to attend. These will not be comfortable things to attend, but they will serve to bring a degree of closure and to that end help in the grieving process. The one form of unexpected death that can be the most difficult to understand is suicide. What would happen if they were a Christian believer? Will they go to heaven?

If a Christian believer has a medical condition, such as cancer, a respiratory, cardiac, or neurological illness and so on, then their death is understood. We do not hesitate in saying, "Absent from the body, present with the Lord." When a professing Christian commits suicide, then there is hesitation. But should there be? If that believer suffered from severe depression, we will never fully realise the depth of darkness and hopelessness they were experiencing. The incessant dark thoughts that they had no control over.

To me, their illness is no different to someone suffering from terminal cancer. The same could be said for other forms of psychotic mental illness such as schizophrenia. Can we begin to understand what it must be like to be driven by paranoid thoughts, voices and hallucinations, day, and night? Despite the best medical efforts, patients with severe depression and psychotic illnesses, take their own lives. Yes, we won't fully understand what has gone on, but in my view, we should not treat them any differently to someone who has died from a physical illness. In the same way, we should comfort the grieving relatives.

In Scripture, Saul, who had begun so well as the first king of Israel, ends very badly. He becomes a proud, impatient, moody individual, disobedient to God and consumed with jealousy regarding David, the teenage shepherd boy, who had in an audacious act of faith killed the Philistine giant, Goliath, and won the admiration of the nation. In fact, he makes David's life extremely difficult, treating him like an enemy, and tries to hunt him down.

Eventually, Saul is wounded in battle, and surrounded by his Philistine enemies, he is fearful of what they might do to him. When his armour bearer refuses to kill him, Saul falls on his own sword—he commits suicide. What is interesting, is David's response to hearing the news of Saul's death. He laments for Saul.

> Therefore, David took hold of his own clothes and tore them, and so did all the men who were with him. And they mourned and wept and fasted until evening for Saul and his son Jonathan, for the people of the Lord and for the house of Israel, because they had fallen by the sword. (2 Samuel 1:11-12)
> Then David lamented with this lamentation over Saul and his son Jonathan… (1 Samuel 1:17-27)

As Amy Orr-Ewing writes, "A truly Christian response to suicide is to show grief and lament. Lament seems to hold together an acknowledgement of the agony with a refusal to deny the goodness of God."[21]

---

[21] Amy Orr-Ewing, *Where Is God in All the Suffering?* The Good Book Company, page 66.

Chapter 10
Forgiveness

One thing is certain in life, and that is, sooner or later, we are going to be hurt by someone. No one plans to get hurt or likes being hurt. However, how we respond to that hurt will have a significant impact on our own well-being. Jesus knew this. When His disciples asked Him to teach them how to pray, He gave them a skeleton prayer, on which they could build their own prayers. At the heart of that prayer is 'forgiveness'.

> Our Father in heaven, hallowed be Your Name. Your kingdom come. Your will be done on earth as it is in heaven. Give us this day our daily bread.
> And forgive us our debts, as we forgive our debtors.
> And do not lead us into temptation but deliver us from the evil one. For Yours is the kingdom and the power and the glory forever. Amen. (Matthew 6:9-13)

To emphasise the subject of forgiveness, Jesus goes onto say, in the verses following:

> For if you forgive men their trespasses, your heavenly Father will also forgive you. But if you do not forgive

men their trespasses, neither will your Father forgive your trespasses. (Matthew 6:14-15)

On another occasion, Peter asks Jesus, "Lord, how often shall my brother sin against me, and I forgive him? Up to seven times?"

Jesus replies, "I do not say to you up to seven times, but up to seventy times seven" (Matthew 18:21-22). Jesus then goes on to share a parable with his disciples. He tells the story of a king who wanted to settle accounts with his servants. One of the first to appear before the king is someone who owed him ten thousand talents (one talent is said to be worth more than 15 years wages of a labourer[22]—say £200,000. Ten thousand talents are going to be £200,000 X 10,000).

In whatever way the value of a talent is calculated, it is a phenomenal debt. As the servant was not able to pay, the king commanded that the man be sold into slavery, along with his wife and children and all that he had. Jesus continues by saying that the man fell down before his master and said, "Master, have patience with me, and I will pay you all." The master was moved with compassion, released him, and forgave him the debt.

What a release of debt. What forgiveness! But Jesus continues the story. The man who has been forgiven such a large debt finds a fellow servant who owes him a hundred denarii (Talmudic scholars say there were six thousand denarii to one talent[23]—say £133 and 100 denarii would be about £2.20).

---

[22] Talent (measurement)—Wikipedia.
[23] Talent (measurement)—Wikipedia.

Jesus says that the man who has just been forgiven such a large debt, grabs the other man by the throat, saying, "Pay me what you owe!" The fellow servant falls down at his feet and begs him, saying, "Have patience with me, and I will pay you all." But the man would not. He threw him into prison till he should pay his debt. Unbelievable!

The fellow servants were grieved by what had happened and reported it to their master. Jesus continues:

> Then the master, after he had called him, said to him, "You wicked servant. I forgave you all that debt because you begged me. Should not you also have had compassion on your fellow servant, just as I had pity on you?"
> And his master was angry and delivered him to the torturers until he should pay all that was due him.
> So, My heavenly Father also will do to you if each of you, from his heart, does not forgive his brother his trespasses. (Matthew 18:21-35)

Unwillingness to forgive, even though he had been forgiven a phenomenal amount, resulted in the first servant being handed over to the torturers.

Jesus is teaching his disciples, and through the Scriptures, us, not only the importance of forgiveness but the consequences of being unforgiving. As those who have been forgiven our enormous debt of sin, through the sacrificial death of Jesus, the Son of God, on the cross, we are expected to forgive those who hurt and offend us. Our hurt is nothing in comparison to our sin which offended a Holy God and is worthy of punishment in eternal hell. To not forgive, is to put ourselves in a place of torture, through resentment and bitterness. Unforgiveness eats away at our innermost being, affecting our thinking, our speaking, and our general and physical well-being.

As Nelson Mandela put it, "Resentment is like drinking poison and waiting for your enemy to die."[24] Nicky Gumbel puts it like this, "Holding a grudge is like allowing someone else to live rent free in your head."[25]

Personal story

The first thirteen and a half years of our pastoral ministry we spent in the South Wales Valley community of Pontllanfraith. God had richly blessed us there and we had seen the church grow from just less than thirty people, meeting in an old tin shack, to touching two hundred in a new church building. We had also planted a church further up the Rhymney Valley. Then the door opened to move to the city of Bristol. This was an exciting new challenge.

We were passionate about prayer, raising leaders and planting churches. In the Pontllanfraith surrounding area, there were a lot of small churches of the same denomination and it had been difficult to plant out without stepping on someone's toes. We saw the city as being made up of many districts and our vision was to see raised up a strong central base church with satellite congregations. We shared this at the

---

[24] Nelson Mandela cited in Phil Cousineau, Beyond Forgiveness: Reflections on Atonement (Jossey-Bass, 2011) p. 139.
[25] Nicky Gumbel, The Bible in One Year (Hodder and Stoughton), Day 68.

interview. In a later interview, which included the church deacons, I used the phrase, "I am not a pastor, pastor."

I was asked by one of the deacons, "What exactly is your ministry?" I replied, "It is to build and plant. Without wishing to sound boastful, it is apostolic in nature." The board of elders and deacons seemed satisfied with my answers and invited us to lead the church, which, at that time, had a congregation of around one hundred and twenty people.

After we had started ministry in Bristol, we were told that the previous pastor had left, having said publicly, that it had been the most difficult years of his ministry. The pastor who had been there before him told me, "The best thing for the church, would be to blow it up and rebuild it!" He was not speaking about the building! Not quite what we wanted to hear.

After a period of settling in, we began to explore reaching out to one of the districts of Bristol. We set up a thriving children's work and then, approaching Christmas, put on a special Christmas service in a school hall in that district. It was exciting. We had over one hundred come to that service. Sadly, the elders were not so excited.

Tensions were beginning to develop. There was a difference of vision that can only be described in one word, 'division'. By that time, we had also taken on a youth pastor who was quite radical and forward-thinking. We knew that to move forward we needed to build a fresh leadership team. I began to share this with the elders.

Then it happened. One morning, I received a letter. In that letter, the elders said that they could not share my vision and they were not happy with the way the church was being led, so they were all resigning and leaving the church. The letter went on to say things about me that were not true. The letter was sent to all the church members, adherents, and many local ministers. It was a huge shock to me and to the church.

As much as we needed a fresh leadership team, this was not the way I intended to go about it! One person told me that I could take legal action. I immediately declined to go down that route. But how was I to respond? I had had challenges before, but nothing like this. I was grateful for the support of my youth pastor, who came from a strong Christian family, his father being a minister, but the bottom line was that I had to somehow sort this out.

It could have been so easy to lash out at those who had now left or to make rash decisions and quickly put people in place to replace those leaders. The congregation needed support. Some left the church—confused by what was going on, whilst others were happy that the church could make a fresh start. I was on an emotional roller coaster, and I had to find a way to deal with the hurt I was experiencing if I was going to be an effective minister and leader to the people. Alongside that, I had a wife and a young family who needed protection in the midst of all that was going on. I was struggling.

Steps to forgiveness

As I prayed and sought the face of God, I began to see that whatever else I did, at the top of the list must come forgiveness. As I prayed this through, I realised that forgiveness was more than just saying the right words or writing letters, it is first and foremost a condition of the heart. I learned that the first step in forgiveness is to come to the cross. I had to spend time meditating on how Jesus forgave me. Without Him, I was lost in my sin and going to a lost eternity.

The moment I called upon Him and asked Him to forgive me of my sins, He did. Not only did He forgive me, but He also declared me righteous, and I became one of His children. This was God's amazing grace. As I began to appreciate, afresh, how Jesus had forgiven me, I was ready for the second step. I could begin to pray, "Lord, help me to forgive, as you forgive. Holy Spirit help me. Fill me with your grace."

The third step to forgiveness was the toughest. The Holy Spirit whispered in my heart, "Now pray God's blessing on each of them and their families." At first, this seemed a little strange and difficult, but the more I did this, the easier it became until I really was wanting God to bless them and their families! I was now at the fourth step, where I not only kept on praying for God's blessing but carried forgiveness in my heart.

I was now at a point, where, if I met any of these individuals and they were to begin to apologise, then I could without hesitation pour out love, forgiveness, and blessing upon them. I saw that this is how it is with God. He constantly carries in His heart the capacity to forgive. We only have to take a small step in asking forgiveness of our sins, and He comes running to us, to forgive us. The prodigal son story (Luke 15:11-24) or the thief on the cross (Luke 23:42-43) are notable examples of God's immediate response to forgive.

The Holy Spirit had not yet finished with me. The Lord put it on my heart that I should visit one of those who were part of the former leadership team. I did, as I felt led, and having arrived at his home, rang the doorbell, but there was no reply. I was quietly relieved! But then a week later, I felt the Holy Spirit urging me to go again. This time his wife was in, but he was out.

I was happy to leave it at that, but again, the Holy Spirit urged me to go back. This time he was in! We chatted. We discussed what happened. It was an 'agreeing to disagree' situation. Before I left, I asked if I could pray for him. He agreed and I was able, without inhibition, to pray God's blessing upon him and the other leaders. As I left his house, I felt as though I was walking on air. I felt God's presence in a powerful way.

From time to time, I have met some of those leaders and their wives. I have been able to greet them and ask about their well-being, without any feeling of animosity. What I have also had to do, is to keep praying blessings, and keep my heart open and ready to forgive, not just them but anyone else who has hurt me or will hurt me in the future! If I did not, then I was well aware that I could relapse into negative thinking and that any small hurt could trigger past hurts.

Bitterness

One of the saddest things in ministry is to see people, once good people, hurt and overcome with bitterness and unforgiveness. Whether it is a broken marriage, an unresolved family dispute, a fallout at work, a breakup of a friendship or just not being able to forgive themselves for something they have said or done, there are a number of reasons why people get hurt. The downside of relationships of any description is the potential for hurt! That said, God has made us for relationships. "It is not good that man should be alone" (Genesis 2:18). Forgiveness is the antidote to hurt.

If the antidote is not applied, then there is, sadly, a downward spiral. By the constant rehearsing of the hurt, staying awake thinking about it, having pity parties, and talking to others about it, the hurt increasingly takes over a person's life. Yes, in the shock of the hurt, we are likely to do those things, but we cannot stay there, we have to start on the road to forgiveness. If not, bitterness sets in and bitterness affects our whole being. In both ministry and medical practice, I have seen people present with physical illness, and when I have begun to dig deeper into their history, hurt and unforgiveness were where it all started.

As I write, I think of a lady who at one time had been truly kind and went out of her way to help people. Then she was hurt, and instead of following the path of forgiveness, went down the road of bitterness. She changed. She became extremely negative and in a matter of just a few years became crippled with arthritis.

I could write down a number of medical conditions that can arise or get worse because of bitterness. I have chosen not to, because I know people will read them and think that is the reason, they are sick. You will know in a brief time spent with a person if their illness is the result of unforgiveness and bitterness. It will not be long before they are 'inviting you to their pity party' and talking about their grievances and all the dreadful things that have been done or said about them.

Communion

In writing to the Corinthians, the Apostle Paul has this to say, about communion:

> Therefore, whoever eats this bread or drinks the cup of the Lord in an unworthy manner will be guilty of the body and blood of the Lord. But let a man (woman) examine himself, and so let him eat of the bread and drink of the cup. For he who eats and drinks in an unworthy manner eats and drinks judgement to himself, not discerning the Lord's body. For this reason, many are weak and sick among you, and many sleep. For if we would judge ourselves, we would not be judged. (1 Corinthians 11:27-31)

As I read these verses, as well as ignoring the poor and needy, there were unresolved relationship problems in the Corinthian church. Despite this, people were continuing to take communion as if there were no problems at all. The result was weakness and sickness and even death. Paul is encouraging them to examine their hearts and put forgiveness into action. James is dealing with the same subject when he writes:

> Is any among you sick? Let him (her) call for the elders of the church, and let them pray over him (her), anointing him (her) with oil in the name of the Lord. And the prayer of faith will save the sick, and the Lord will raise him up. And if he (she) has committed sins, he (she) will be forgiven.

> Confess your trespasses to one another, and pray for one another, that you may be healed. (James 5:14-16)

When conducting communion, our concern should be, not so much about some unbelievers, out of ignorance taking the communion emblems, but of believers living in unresolved broken relationships and unforgiveness. Those of us who are leaders should be constantly teaching and reminding our people of the importance and benefits to our own well-being of forgiveness. And yes, of course, we should explain what the communion is all about and invite any unbelievers present to come to Christ!

As you read this chapter, you might be saying to yourself, "But the person who caused me great hurt has moved away or even died. What should I do?" The steps that I set out earlier can still be applied. First and foremost, forgiveness is a condition of the heart.

Coming before the cross, confessing your faults, seeing how Christ has forgiven you, asking for His help to forgive and praying for blessing on them (if the person has died blessing on his/her family), still applies. Get your heart free! If you struggle, then pray with others you can trust—but do not hold a pity party!

Where a person who has caused hurt, broke the law in causing that hurt, then as part of the forgiveness process, we can surrender justice to the Lord and those He has appointed to minister justice.

> "Vengeance is Mine, I will repay," says the Lord. (Romans 12:19, Deuteronomy 32:35)

> Let everyone be subject to the governing authorities. For there is no authority except from God, and the authorities that exist are appointed by God.
>
> For he is God's minister to you for good. But if you do evil, be afraid. For he does not bear the sword in vain, for he is God's minister, an avenger to execute wrath on him who practices evil. (Romans 13:1, 4)

The trial and crucifixion of Jesus was a huge miscarriage of justice, yet Jesus' first words from the cross were, "Father, forgive them, for they do not know what they do" (Luke 23:34).

Chapter 11
Demons

The subject of demons is not an easy one to write about. As a generalisation, the Western worldview is 'scientifically based'. Things must be seen to be believed, whilst the Eastern worldview is more open to the spiritual world and things do not have to be seen to be believed. Talking to friends from India, they will readily bring the 'spirit world' into their conversation, but you would not usually hear stories like that from people who were born and brought up in the west.

In Christian circles, in my experience, there are two opposite camps. One camp virtually denies the existence of demons, whilst the other camp has an over-fascination with them, and demons are blamed for almost everything! Certainly, in the ministry of Jesus, the Gospels are filled with incidents of Jesus casting out demons. Here are two examples, from many, in the Gospels.

> Now there was a man in the synagogue with an unclean spirit. And he cried out, saying, "Let us alone! What have we to do with You, Jesus of Nazareth? Did you come to destroy us? I know who You are—the Holy One of God!"

But Jesus rebuked him, saying, "Be quiet, and come out of him!"

And when the unclean spirit had convulsed him and cried out with a loud voice, he came out of him. Then they were all amazed, so that they questioned among themselves, saying, "What is this? What new doctrine is this? For with authority, He commands even the unclean spirits, and they obey Him." (Mark 1:23-27).

When evening had come, they brought to Him many who were demon-possessed. And He cast out the spirits with a word and healed all who were sick. (Matthew 8:16)

The origin of demons

You might be asking, "If there are demons, where did they come from?" To answer that question, we must go back to the creation of angelic beings. Reading Scripture, there would appear to be three groups of angelic beings. One group are the messenger angels, led by the archangel Gabriel. Gabriel, himself features in the nativity story, appearing to Mary to tell her that she is going to conceive and bring forth a Son, who she is to call Jesus (Luke 1:26-38). He also brings a message to Daniel about future kings and empires and events (Daniel 8:16-26, 9:21-27).

Around the throne of God, there are angelic creatures (seraphim) who appear to be messenger angels. In Isaiah chapter six, Isaiah has a vision of God's throne, and he sees these angels, each with six wings—two to cover their face, two to cover their feet and two with which to fly—ready to do the bidding of God.

Another group are the warrior angels, led by the archangel Michael. Daniel has been praying and fasting for twenty-one days, waiting for an answer to prayer:

> Suddenly, a hand touched me, which made me tremble on my knees and on the palms of my hands. And he said to me, "o Daniel, man greatly beloved, understand the words that I speak to you, and stand upright, for I have now been sent to you." Whilst he was speaking this word to me, I stood trembling. Then he said to me, "Do not fear, Daniel, for from the first day that you set your heart to understand, and to humble yourself before your God, your words were heard; and I have come because of your words. But the prince of the kingdom of Persia withstood me twenty-one days; and behold Michael, one of the chief princes, came to help me, for I had been left alone there with the kings of Persia. Now I have come to make you understand what will happen to your people in the latter days, for the vision refers to many days yet to come." (Daniel 10:10-14)

Michael gets a further mention in the letter of Jude (Jude 1:9) where he is referred to as Michael the archangel, and in Revelation, it speaks of Michael and his angels fighting against the dragon. (Revelation 12:7)

The third group of angels are led by Lucifer, a beautiful archangel, who had the task of leading the praise and worship in heaven. Ezekiel prophesies of him:

"You were the seal of perfection, full of wisdom and perfect in beauty. You were in Eden, the garden of God; every precious stone was your covering: the sardius, topaz, and diamond, beryl, onyx and jasper, sapphire, turquoise, and emerald with gold. The workmanship of your timbrels and pipes was prepared for you on the day you were created. You were the anointed cherub who covers." (Ezekiel 28:12-14)

Note from these verses, Lucifer's beauty, and his covering of precious jewels. As he stood in God's presence, leading the worship of God, those jewels were to reflect all the glory back to God. Note as well, the musical ability built into Lucifer— the workmanship of your timbrels and pipes. Isaiah, in prophesying about Lucifer, adds, "the sound of your stringed instruments" (Isaiah 14:11). Percussion, wind, and stringed instruments—a keyboard of sound!

As with man, God created angels with free will. He does not want robots worshipping Him. He wants angels and people, to want to worship of their own free will. Lucifer was no exception, except he realised how good he was and, when he saw his own reflection, how splendid he looked. Pride filled his being, and he wanted to be worshipped just like God. Ezekiel prophesies:

> You were perfect in all your ways from the day you were created, till iniquity was found in you. By the abundance of your trading, you became filled with violence within, and you sinned; therefore, I cast you as a profane thing out of the mountain of God; and I

destroyed you, O covering cherub, from the midst of the fiery stones.

Your heart was lifted up because of your beauty; you corrupted your wisdom for the sake of your splendour, I laid you before kings that they might gaze at you. (Ezekiel 28:15-17)

Isaiah prophesies about the same fall in these words:

How you are fallen from heaven, O Lucifer, son of the morning! How you are cut down to the ground, you who weakened the nations! For you have said in your heart: "I will ascend into heaven, I will exalt my throne above the starts of God; I will also sit on the mount of the congregation on the farthest sides of the north; I will ascend above the heights of the clouds, I will be like the Most High." Yet you shall be brought down to Sheol, to the lowest depths of the Pit. (Isaiah 14:12-15)

Jesus spoke of this fall. "I saw Satan fall like lightning from heaven" (Luke 10:18). In Revelation chapter twelve, we have a further description of Lucifer's (Satan's) fall.

And war broke out in heaven: Michael and his angels fought with the dragon; and the dragon and his angels fought, but they did not prevail, nor was a place found for them in heaven any longer. So, the great dragon was cast out, that serpent of old, called the Devil and Satan, who deceives the whole world; he was cast to the earth, and his angels were cast out with him. (Revelation 12:7-9)

From this description, we see that Lucifer (also known as the Devil, Satan, the Dragon, the Serpent, the Deceiver) was thrown out of heaven along with his angels. Assuming each archangel had the same number of angels, then it is likely one-third of all angels followed Lucifer/the Devil. These fallen angelic spirit beings take up their residence in a 'middle heaven' zone. From there, they begin to exert their influence over territories and people groups on earth. Paul the Apostle writes:

> For we do not wrestle against flesh and blood, but against principalities, against power, against the rulers of the darkness of this age, against spiritual hosts of wickedness in the heavenly places. (Ephesians 6:12)

We have already seen in the book of Daniel how Michael fought against the kings of Persia. These were not literal kings but demonic principalities and powers exerting their influence over that region. These fallen angels look to exert influence over areas and people groups, primarily by strongholds of thinking, opposing all that God has said is good. So God Himself, creation, mankind—male and female created in the image of God with creative and moral standing, marriage, Israel, and the church are going to come under attack through thought systems, religious and political that want to undermine God and His plans for the people He loves.

At an individual level, where an individual opens him or herself up to their influence, then these spirit beings first begin to control the mind of a person and as the person yields to their influence, they take control of the very spirit of that individual. This control may affect a person's mood—with very dark moods and possible severe depression; behaviour—immoral behaviour and sexual deviance; language—foul language, altered voice and physical being—resulting in illness or physical deformity. The New Testament talks about—unclean spirits (e.g. Matthew 10:1, Mark 1:27, 3:11, Acts 5:16), evil spirits (Luke 7:21, 8:2, Acts 19:12), demons causing someone to be mute (Matthew 9:32-33, Mark 9:17-18, Luke 11:14), blind and mute (Matthew 12:22), the spirit of infirmity (Luke 13:11-13) and the spirit of divination (Acts 16:16).

The Old Testament talks about familiar spirits (Leviticus 19:31, 20:6). A person may be possessed by one or many (Mark 5:9, Matthew 12:45, Mark 16:9). In the case of the demoniac of Gadara, we get a glimpse of the sorry and depraved state a person possessed by demons is reduced to.

> Then they came to the other side of the sea, to the country of the Gadarenes. And when He (Jesus) came out of the boat, immediately there met Him out of the tombs a man with an unclean spirit, who had been dwelling among the tombs; and no one could bind him, not even with chains, because he had often been bound with shackles and chains. And the chains had been pulled apart by him, and the shackles broken in pieces; neither could anyone tame him. And always night and day, he was in the mountains and the tombs,

crying out and cutting himself with stones. (Mark 5:1-5)

How he got into that state, we are not told. Wild, uncontrolled behaviour, superhuman strength, a fascination with death, crying out in torment and self-harming are some of the destructive features of demon possession in this man. He, in himself, was desperate to be set free, and when Jesus arrived in this place, he ran to Jesus, fell down, and worshipped Him. Jesus sets him free. The demons, which are many, request to go into a herd of pigs, which in turn run into the lake and are drowned. The next that we read of the man, he is sitting and clothed in his right mind! (Mark 5:6-15).

The process of demonisation

As far back as the Old Testament, God warned His people to keep away from mediums and familiar spirits (spirits that are familiar with a deceased person and are able to give false messages, as if they are originating from the deceased person).

> Give no regard to mediums and familiar spirits; do not seek after them, to be defiled by them: I am the Lord your God. (Leviticus 19:31)

And the person who turns to mediums and familiar spirits, to prostitute himself with them, I will set My face against that person and cut him off from his people. (Leviticus 20:6).

God also warned His people not to engage in the idol, Baal and Asherah (the female version of Baal) worship and occult practices of the Canaanite nations. Behind that worship and practice were strong demonic influences, resulting in all manner of sexual perversion, child sacrifice and violence.

The process of demonisation begins with an individual having a fascination with those things. Once the demons get a foothold in a person's mind, the process only deepens until the demons have a grip on a person, spirit, soul, and body. Note that it begins with the mind—with thoughts. We get an example of the battle for the mind way back in the Garden of Eden. Satan in the form of the serpent comes to Eve (Adam is standing close by) and says, "Has God indeed said, 'You shall not eat of every tree of the garden'?"

When the woman replies that they can eat of all the trees of the garden, except for the tree in the midst of the garden, because God has said that if they eat of it, they shall die. Then Satan said, "You shall not surely die. For God knows that in the day you eat of it your eyes will be opened, and you will be like God, knowing good and evil." Subtle, deceptive. Eve then looks at the fruit and sees that it looks beautiful, good to eat and desirable to make one wise, and she takes it, eats it, and gives some to her husband. (Genesis 3:1-6).

Note the fall of man began with thoughts and suggestions. Satan even tried the same technique on Jesus. When Jesus had fasted 40 days, he was physically weak, and his body was craving for food. Satan comes to Jesus and says, "If you are the Son of God, command that these stones become bread."

Jesus answers, "It is written, 'Man shall not live by bread alone, but by every word that proceeds from the mouth of God'." Note that the temptation begins with a doubt and then a suggestion. It is similar to the next two temptations

(Matthew 4:1-11). A battle for the mind, which Jesus overcomes each time by using the word of God.

Paul addresses the battle for the mind in his second letter to the Corinthians and in his letter to the Ephesians.

> For the weapons of our warfare are not carnal but mighty in God for pulling down strongholds, casting down arguments and every high thing that exalts itself against the knowledge of God, bringing every thought into captivity to the obedience of Christ, and being ready to punish every disobedience when your obedience is fulfilled. (2 Corinthians 10:4-6)
>
> Put on the whole armour of God, that you may be able to stand against the wiles of the devil. (Ephesians 6:11)

Entry points to the occult can seem innocent, just new-age thinking and harmless suggestions. The Garden of Eden story shows us otherwise. Horoscopes, tarot cards and Ouija boards may seem harmless to some but by thoughts and suggestions they can become the pathway to becoming demonised. Fortune-telling, certain types of heavy metal music, mediums, Eastern mysticism, paganism, and witchcraft are more obvious pathways. Alongside these practices could be included pornography and drug addiction, which the powers of darkness can certainly use to control and ensnare individuals. The deeper a person goes, the more ensnared and demonised a person becomes.

Release

Jesus set people free from demons and the disciples were given power and authority to do so. Can we do the same? The short answer is, "Yes, we can!" That said, we can only do so, if, our lives are clean and pure (we are not to be double agents—living for God, whilst living for this world!), we know that we have received power and authority and the person we are ministering to is willing to be set free. Let us deal with these points. Paul, in writing to the Ephesians, says:

> Be strong in the Lord and in the power of His might.
> (Ephesians 6:10)

To be strong in the Lord, we must know who we are in Christ. That our sin has been washed away that we have been declared righteous and set apart by the blood of Jesus, and that we are the children of God. As we continue to read on, in Ephesians chapter six, Paul tells us to 'stand' and to put on the whole armour of God—waist girded with truth, the breastplate of righteousness, feet shod with the preparation of the Gospel of peace, the shield of faith, the helmet of salvation and the sword of the Spirit. In a few words, the armour of God could be summarised as our Christian character and witness.

Alongside our armour, we have our weapons. In his second letter to the Corinthians, Paul says that the weapons of our warfare are not carnal but mighty in God. (2 Corinthians 10:4). These weapons are the Word of God (Matthew 4:4, 7,10, Ephesians 6:17), the Blood of Jesus (Revelations 12:11, Romans 5:9, 1 John 1:7), and the Name of Jesus (Philippians 2:9-11).

We must familiarise ourselves with these weapons—just like a soldier in the natural. It is by knowing our weapons and submitting to the Lordship of Jesus, we have our authority. Fasting can certainly be an important part of preparation (Matthew 17:21). In fasting we humble ourselves (our flesh), surrender ourselves to the Lord, listen to His voice, and seek His strength.

Then Paul writes, 'of the power of His might'. This refers to being filled with the Holy Spirit. A one-off experience is not enough. We need to keep on being filled with the Holy Spirit (Ephesians 5:18)—by praise, prayer, and worship. Not only does the Holy Spirit empower us, but one of the gifts of the Spirit is the discerning of spirits and this discernment can be especially useful in knowing what we are dealing with (is it demon spirits, a human spirit, angelic spirits or Holy Spirit?).

Regarding the person who is to be set free, they must be willing. We cannot work contrary to a person's will. God does not do that with us, and we should not do that to others. Even the uncontrollable demoniac of Gadara came to Jesus and worshipped Him (Mark 5:1-15).

Stories of so-called exorcisms going horribly wrong are usually because the person was not willing or those seeking to do the exorcism were not properly prepared or did not have the authority to do so (Acts 19:13-16). When confronted by a person troubled by demon activity, we need to ask the question, "Do you want to be set free?"

John Wimber, in his book, *Power Healing*, says "Prayer for the severely demonised is best accomplished in teams of two to five people. There should be a clearly defined leader, with the others lending prayer support and some counsel."[26]

As you begin to pray, and the Holy Spirit begins to move in the situation, there may be a demonic manifestation. In this situation, we take authority, in Jesus's name, and command the demon(s) to leave. The person may collapse or even convulse. Keep on praying (praying in the Spirit) until you discern a real sense of peace. Then, in that Spirit-filled atmosphere, challenge the person to declare, "Jesus Christ is Lord."

If they struggle to declare the Lordship of Jesus, continue praying and then ask them again. When they are freely able to do that, invite them to pray, renouncing all of the activities that may have led them to become demonised in the first place and then invite Jesus to become their Lord and Saviour. Whenever possible, go a step further, and pray with them to be filled with the Holy Spirit. This may seem a lot to take in, so let me share some first-hand experiences.

Experiences

One of my first experiences occurred in the first few years of my being a pastor. We had had a remarkably busy Sunday. God had been moving in the meetings and by the evening, I was glad to start relaxing and unwinding. It was then that I had a phone call. On the line was a person crying out for help.

He (we shall call him, Pete—not his real name) in a distressed voice spoke of how something kept coming over him, making him do strange things, and act in strange ways.

---

[26] John Wimber, Power Healing (Hodder and Stoughton), page 240.

Pete went on to say that his wife had fled the house that day, scared by what she saw happening to him. You could almost detect the turmoil he was in, on the phone, and he asked me to go to his house and help him. I agreed, took his address, and went to see him. My first mistake!

On the way, I began to question myself about what I was doing. I said to myself, "Rob, you should have asked someone to go with you. Why didn't you make an appointment to see him at the church, the next day, when you could have been better prepared?" Too late, I was on my way.

I arrived at Pete's house. He invited me in, and I at once began to discern that something spiritually was very wrong. My second mistake was to sit down on a chair away from the door. Pete was between me and the door. I was trapped! Pete's manner and behaviour began to change, and his eyes took on a sinister look. At that moment, I could not look him in the eyes.

So I closed mine and began, out loud, to pray in the Spirit (in tongues). I prayed like this for between thirty minutes and an hour, then I felt an extremely powerful anointing of the Holy Spirit come upon me. I commanded the demonic influence to leave Pete and leave the house. In a moment, Pete became peaceful, and his demeanour changed.

I prayed with him. I then told him to go to a church on a Monday evening, where I knew they had a prayer meeting, and introduce himself to the minister (someone senior to me and vastly more experienced than me). I then left.

Pete did what I said. At that prayer meeting, he accepted Christ as his Saviour. When I spoke to the minister and explained what had happened, he reassured me that Pete was at peace and there was no further manifestation of demon activity. The next Sunday, Pete attended the church that I led in Pontllanfraith, and came to lunch with my wife and family afterwards!

During my time of ministry in Pontllanfraith, we saw God move in an amazing way amongst young people. One of the young people who came to Christ was Phil. Phil, prior to his conversion, had been using drugs, including the hallucinogenic drug LSD. One of the problems with LSD is that people who have been taking it can get flashbacks for some years later. One night, Phil was at the youth leader's home along with many of the young people, when he experienced a severe flashback.

He imagined that the people in the room were monsters. The images to him were very real, and he began screaming and thrashing out and tried to escape the room. The other young people began to pray extra loud for him. Some tried to restrain him. That just made him worse! The youth leader phoned me.

I quickly went over to the youth leader's home. On arrival, Phil was in a terrible state. I told everyone to be quiet. I then very quietly began to pray for Phil. I discerned that Satan was making the most of Phil's situation.

I asked him to declare, "Jesus is Lord." When, at first, he tried, he could not form the words. It was as if something was stopping him. I prayed again, quietly commanding the powers of darkness to let go of Phil. I asked him, once again, to declare the Lordship of Jesus.

This time, with a struggle, he managed to. I prayed some more. On the third time, he was able to declare freely, "Jesus Christ is Lord." I then prayed for him to be filled with the

Holy Spirit. Very quickly, he was filled with the Holy Spirit and began speaking in other tongues.

On another occasion, an older lady, who had been attending the church for just a few weeks, began to behave strangely in the middle of a service, shaking and making noises. The presence of God was very real in the meeting, and I discerned that this was a demonic manifestation. I did not know the lady's background and did not know whether she was willing to be set free. What I did do was to take authority, in Jesus's name, and command the manifestation to stop. It stopped at that very moment, and she was peaceful for the rest of the service. Afterwards, she was unwilling to receive ministry.

It is not unusual for demonic manifestations to occur when God is moving. Whether the individual wants to be set free or not, we have the authority to command them to be quiet. It is better for any deliverance ministry, if the person is willing, to take place away from the main meeting.

When Paul the Apostle visited Philippi, the Scripture records:

> Now it happened, as we went to prayer, that a certain slave girl possessed with a spirit of divination met us, who brought her masters much profit by fortune-telling. This girl followed Paul and us, and cried out, saying, "These men are the servants of the Most High God, who proclaim to us the way of salvation." And this she did for many days. But Paul, greatly annoyed, turned, and said to the spirit, "I command you in the name of Jesus Christ to come out of her." And he came out that very hour. (Acts 16:16-18)

The slave girl was saying the right things, but it was a demonic distraction, and after a couple of days, Paul recognised this, took authority, and commanded the spirit to leave!

Mental illness

One of the challenges that ministers face is knowing when something is due to a mental illness and when something is due to demons. For a season in ministry, other pastors were referring individuals to me, they were not sure about. This was because I was both a doctor and a pastor. It was not something that I was advertising to do!

When an individual is constantly battling with episodes of depression associated with dark thoughts or an individual has been diagnosed as having schizophrenia and is constantly hearing voices and behaving in bizarre ways, it is easy to understand why some would label those individuals as being demon-possessed. To that list, some would add epilepsy. I am pleased that, at least in the case of epilepsy, Matthew makes a differentiation.

> Then His fame went throughout all Syria; and they brought to Him all sick people who were afflicted with various diseases and torments, and those who were demon-possessed, epileptics, and paralytics; and He healed them. (Matthew 4:24)

Note that Matthew does not put those with epilepsy in the same category as those who were demon-possessed. Very simply, epilepsy is a condition where there is abnormal electrical activity across the surface of the brain. This can, from time to time, depending on the type of epilepsy, set off a convulsive episode. Such convulsions are not to be confused with the convulsions a person gripped by demons may manifest when they encounter the power of God.

Matthew also distinguishes people with 'torments'. Could this be people who were tormented by mental illness, as opposed to demons? Just like epilepsy can be due to abnormal electrical activity, some mental health conditions can be due to a lack of chemical transmitters or disruption of thought processing in the brain.

When I was asked to see an individual, I would spend time beforehand in prayer. When the person arrived for the appointment, after the initial conversation of getting to know them, I would ask them if they knew why their pastor had referred them and if they were happy to discuss this further. It would be a waste of time to proceed with something they were not willing to deal with. If they were willing, then I would begin by getting what I would call, 'their spiritual history'.

Questions I would want to cover included such things as: Have they accepted Christ as Saviour? What sort of things were they involved with in the past? Was there any occult involvement? Were any close family members involved with the occult? What kind of music do they listen to? What sort of films do they watch? What are their views on horoscopes and fortune-telling? How these questions were answered would give me an indication as to what may be going on.

Alongside this, I would get a mental health history. When did the condition start? What was going on in their life at the time? How does it affect them (things such as mood, motivation, concentration, eating, sleeping, self-care, relationship to others and suicidal thoughts)? At what times does it affect them the most? And so on.

We would then move to a time of prayer. I would explain that we would be spending some time in prayer and praise, waiting on the Holy Spirit. Throughout this process, I would have someone who was very prayerful with me. We would spend some time exalting and praising the Lord Jesus, declaring that He is Lord and that in His name, every knee must bow. In that spiritual atmosphere, I would ask the person to declare that 'Jesus Christ is Lord'.

If at that point there was resistance, or they found it difficult to do so, then it was likely that there was a demonic influence present. We would pray some more and command what was binding them to be loosed. I would then ask them to say once again, "Jesus is Lord." Once they were able to freely declare, 'Jesus is Lord', then I would ask them to renounce the works of darkness that they had been involved with, and if they were not already a Christian, to accept Christ as Saviour. We would then go on to pray for them to be filled with the Holy Spirit.

It must be emphasised that throughout the complete process, the person being ministered to, must be willing to proceed. Where there was no occult involvement, where I did not discern any demonic activity and where the person freely and easily confessed 'Jesus is Lord', then I would reassure them and pray for them to be healed of their mental health condition. If they were to continue to have struggles with their mental health, then I would advise them that they should not be embarrassed to get psychiatric help.

Chapter 12
Power to Heal the Sick

The Gospels not only tell us how Jesus healed the sick, but how He sent out His disciples to do the same.

> And when He had called His twelve disciples to Him, He gave them power over unclean spirits, to cast them out, and to heal all kinds of sickness and all kinds of disease. (Matthew 10:1)
> And as you go, preach, saying, "The kingdom of heaven is at hand." Heal the sick, cleanse the lepers, raise the dead, cast out demons. Freely you have received, freely give. (Matthew 10:7-8)

As Jesus was preparing His disciples for the time when He would now longer physically be with them, He said to them:

> Most assuredly, I say to you, he who believes in Me, the works that I do he will do also: and greater works than these he will do, because I go to My Father. (John 14:12)

There has been much discussion about what 'greater works' may mean. My view is that it means greater in terms of volume. Whereas Jesus, as the Son of God become flesh, was restricted, in His earthly ministry, to one place at a time, now through multitudes of believers, filled with the Holy Spirit, His works are being performed right across the Globe. The Acts of the Apostles (better entitled, the Acts of the Holy Spirit), is a testament to that. The commission to believers, as given at the end of Mark's Gospel, says:

> Go into all the world and preach the Gospel to every creature. He who believes and is baptised will be saved; but he who does not believe will be condemned. And these signs will follow those who believe: In My Name they will cast out demons; they will speak with new tongues... They will lay hands on the sick, and they will recover. (Mark 16:15-18)

Mark concludes his Gospel, by saying, "And they went out and preached everywhere, the Lord working with them and confirming the word through the accompanying signs." (Mark 16:20). I love the use of the word, 'signs'. Healings and miracles are not to be an end in themselves, but signposts directing people to Jesus!

As Luke begins writing the Acts of the Apostles (what in effect is his second letter to a nobleman by the name of Theophilus[27]), he writes that his Gospel was just the beginning of what Jesus began to do and teach (Acts 1:1). In other words, with the coming of the Holy Spirit, we have the

---

[27] Luke 1:1-4, Acts 1:1.

continuation of Jesus ministry through the lives of Spirit-filled believers. If we, in our day and generation, are going to be part of that ongoing ministry, then we too, must be filled with the Holy Spirit.

Baptism in the Holy Spirit

Whether we refer to being filled with the Holy Spirit or being baptised in the Holy Spirit, matters not, as they are one and the same experience. So how can I be filled? To help us answer that question, consider the one hundred and twenty in the upper room. Jesus had spoken in depth, (John chapters 14-16), at the time of the Last Supper, that He would be sending the Holy Spirit (the Comforter/Helper) and that having the Holy Spirit would be just like having Him with them. Then, prior to His ascension to heaven, Jesus told them:

> Behold, I send you the Promise of My Father upon you; but tarry in the city of Jerusalem until you are endued with power from on high. (Luke 24:49)

The word endued could be translated as clothed. Clothed with power from on high. As we move to the first chapter of Acts, Luke writes:

> And being assembled together with them, He commanded them not to depart from Jerusalem, but to wait for the Promise of the Father, 'which', He said, "you have heard from Me; for John truly baptised with water, but you shall be baptised with

the Holy Spirit not many days from now" (Acts 1:4-5)

But you shall receive power when the Holy Spirit has come upon you, and you shall be witnesses to Me in Jerusalem, and in all Judea and Samaria, and to the end of the earth. (Acts 1:8)

The first thing I want us to notice is that they had a promise from the Lord Himself. This promise is ours too! Peter in explaining what had happened on the Day of Pentecost, says:

For the promise is to you and your children, and to all who are afar off, as many as the Lord our God will call. (Acts 2:39)

We have a heavenly Father who longs (more than we will ever realise) to give us the gift of the Holy Spirit. If you then, being evil (in comparison to God[28]), know how to give good gifts to your children, how much more will your heavenly Father give the Holy Spirit to those who ask Him! (Luke 11:13)

As we begin to seek God for the baptism in the Holy Spirit, we should do so with eager anticipation and expectancy! This is what the hundred and twenty were doing. Along with expectancy, the posture of their hearts was also ready to receive.

---

[28] My words.

> And they worshipped Him, and returned to Jerusalem with great joy, and were continually in the temple praising and blessing God. (Luke 24:52-53) These all continued with one accord in prayer and supplication. (Acts 1:14)

Worship, joyful expectation, praise, blessing God, prayer, and supplication, are all expressions that tell us of the posture of their hearts in getting ready to receive the Holy Spirit. Nothing has changed! If you are a believer in Jesus, then with joyful expectation start praising and praying, lifting your heart and hands in worship. Vocalise your praise and begin to 'drink in' the presence of God.

As wave after wave of the Holy Spirit floods into and over your being, then do not be surprised if you find yourself praising God in a new language! The words might sound like repeated syllables at first (think about it, that is what a toddler does when they start speaking), but as you speak you will become more articulate until the language you are speaking will have the rise and flow of a normal language. As Jesus said, "From your innermost being there will flow rivers of living water" (John 7:38).

On the Day of Pentecost, they were all filled with the Holy Spirit and began to speak with other tongues as the Spirit gave them utterance. (Acts 2:4). Why tongues? There are several reasons. Firstly, when the Holy Spirit came upon people in the Old Testament, and even in the New Testament, prior to Pentecost, people spoke in their known language—they prophesied. Examples include:

> Then the Lord came down, and spoke to him (Moses), and took of the Spirit that was upon him, and placed the same upon the seventy elders; and it happened, that they prophesied, although they never did so again. (Numbers 11:25)
>
> Then the Spirit of the Lord will come upon you, and you will prophesy with them and be turned into another man. (1 Samuel 10:6)
>
> Now his father Zacharias was filled with the Holy Spirit and prophesied. (Luke 1:67)

From Pentecost onwards, as well as prophesying, there is a new sign and that is speaking in other tongues (Acts 2:4, 10:44-46, Acts 19:6). This new sign is a constant reminder that we are in a new age where the commission is to go into the entire world (not just Israel) and share the good news with every tribe, tongue, people, and nation. Secondly, speaking in tongues is so valuable in our personal prayer and praise. For example, when we are burdened about something and are not sure how to pray, we can pray in the Spirit, until the burden lifts. I am sure that the Apostle Paul, who daily had the burden of his co-workers and churches on his heart, had this in mind when he says:

> I thank my God I speak with tongues more than you all. (1 Corinthians 14:18)
>
> Likewise, the Spirit also helps in our weaknesses. For we do not know what we should pray for as we ought, but the Spirit Himself makes intercession for us with groanings which cannot be uttered. Now He who searches the hearts knows what the mind of the Spirit

is, because He makes intercession for the saints according to the will of God. (Romans 8:26-27)

In praise, we can sing with the Spirit and sing with the understanding also. (1 Corinthians 14:15, Colossians 3:16).

A third reason speaking/praying in tongues is so beneficial, is that it tunes our hearts to the Holy Spirit. I find this really useful when I am praying for people. I can quietly pray in tongues, and as I do the Holy Spirit prompts me as to how I should pray for the individual or cause me to be used in one of the gifts of the Holy Spirit. (1 Corinthians 12:8-10). Worshipping and praising in the language of the Spirit, opens up my heart to receive more of the Holy Spirit. It is so important that we are filled and continually refilled with the Holy Spirit. Paul, writing to the Ephesians, says:

> And do not be drunk with wine, in which is dissipation; but be filled (continually filled) with the Spirit, speaking to one another in psalms and hymns and spiritual songs, singing and making melody in your heart to the Lord, giving thanks always for all things to God the Father in the name of our Lord Jesus Christ. (Ephesians 5:18-20)

Note Paul's emphasis on worship and praise. God comes to dwell where people are praising Him. Also note Paul's comparison to the alcoholic—someone who cannot live without alcohol. From morning to evening that person needs to have a drink. Paul is saying do not be alcoholics but be 'Spiritolics'—needing the Holy Spirit constantly, not able to live without Him. It is He who empowers us. It is He who enables us to be powerful witnesses for Jesus. (Acts 1:8).

In the Acts of the Apostles, 40% of the time, individuals received without anyone laying hands on them, and 60% of the recorded times, individuals received with the laying on of hands. It matters not which way we receive the filling of the Holy Spirit, so long as we receive and keep on receiving! What is more, we go deeper and deeper in our experience of the Holy Spirit. In Ezekiel chapter forty-seven, Ezekiel has a vision of a river flowing from the altar of God. He describes waters to the knees, waters to the ankles, waters to the waist and waters to swim in. The river is the river of God, the Holy Spirit, and may we all get to that place where we are totally abandoned to the Holy Spirit—swimming in the Spirit!

One of the first times, in John's Gospel that Jesus speaks of the Holy Spirit, He says:

> "If anyone thirsts, let him come to Me and drink. He who believes in Me, as the Scripture has said, out of his heart (from his innermost being) will flow rivers of living water." But this He spoke concerning the Spirit, whom those believing in Him would receive. (John 7:37-39)

Note the expression, rivers. One source, many rivers. This refers to the fruit of the Spirit (Galatians 5:22) and the gifts of the Holy Spirit (1 Corinthians 12:4-11). As Spirit-filled believers, not only should we manifest the fruit of the Spirit (love, joy, peace, longsuffering, kindness, goodness, faithfulness, gentleness, and self-control), but we should flow in the gifts of the Spirit.

Gifts of the Holy Spirit

Listed in 1 Corinthians 12 are nine gifts of the Holy Spirit. The source for all of them is the Holy Spirit.

> For to one is given the word of wisdom through the Spirit, to another the word of knowledge through the same Spirit, to another faith by the same Spirit, to another gifts of healings by the same Spirit, to another working of miracles, to another prophecy, to another discerning of spirits, to another different kinds of tongues, to another the interpretation of tongues. But one and the same Spirit works all these things, distributing to each one individually as He wills. (1 Corinthians 12:8-11)

Whilst I want to concentrate on those gifts related to healing, it is useful to get a general overview of all the gifts. For the sake of study, the gifts can be divided into three groups of three. This is useful for study, but, in practice, there will be a lot of overlap. This should not surprise us, as there is one source, and that is the person of the Holy Spirit. So, for study purposes only, we have three vocal gifts—different kinds of tongues, the interpretation of tongues and prophecy; three revelation gifts—word of wisdom, word of knowledge, and discerning of spirits; three demonstration gifts—faith, healings, and working of miracles. Let us quickly look at them.

We have already looked at the wonderful benefit of speaking in tongues, praying, and praising in tongues for our own personal edification (1 Corinthians 14:4). Then there are moments, usually in a gathering of believers, when the Holy

Spirit moves someone, to give a message in tongues. In an atmosphere of the Holy Spirit, believers' hearts are quickened, and wait to hear the interpretation of that message. There may be two or three such messages, each followed by an interpretation (1 Corinthians 14:27). The interpretation may not be an exact translation, but rather an explanation of the 'message' in tongues.

I remember being in an all-night prayer meeting and someone gave a message in tongues in Latin. My Latin, from school days, was rusty, but I could make out the gist of the message. It was a real blessing to hear the person give the interpretation (someone who had never studied Latin in his life)—and it was in keeping with the message! Such messages in tongues, with the corresponding interpretations, can not only be a way of encouraging God's people but also a means of generating and inspiring faith. This includes faith for healing.

Another of the vocal gifts is prophecy. Paul was very keen that the church at Corinth should pursue this gift.

> Pursue love, and desire spiritual gifts, but especially that you may prophecy. (1 Corinthians 14:1)

When a Spirit-filled believer is used in prophecy, the Spirit moves them (2 Peter 1:21) to give a message in the known language. Such a message may be words that God gives or the description of a vision (picture) that God lays on their heart and mind. In whatever form the prophecy comes, Paul says that it will have one of three effects.

> He who prophesies speaks edification and exhortation and comfort to men. (1 Corinthians 14:3)

Prophecy edifies—it builds up; exhorts—inspires and challenges; comforts—tenderly loves and cares. However, as a Spirit-filled believer, becomes increasingly sensitive to the Holy Spirit, then there may be overlap with other gifts of the Holy Spirit such as words of knowledge and words of wisdom, and the words themselves may inspire faith!

God is the all-wise God and a word of wisdom is where, by the Holy Spirit, we are given a fragment of that wisdom (advice, counsel) to pass onto someone else. A word of wisdom could form part of a prophecy or be a word that you are given to pass on to someone who, for example, is struggling in some way and needs an answer. This gift is certainly not exclusive to the church. It could be, for example, that an unsaved work colleague is struggling in some way. You note this and start praying for him/her.

As you pray, God gives you a word of wisdom showing you not only what the struggle is (that is a word of knowledge) but Divine advice and counsel in how to deal with it. Imagine sharing such a word with your colleague! I am quite sure that they would be blessed, but even better, drawn to God through that word.

God knows everything, past, present, and future. There is nothing hidden from Him. A word of knowledge is a fragment of that Divine all-knowingness revealed to us by the Holy Spirit. In ministering in a congregational setting, words of knowledge, used to identify specific sicknesses and pains, can be a powerful encouragement for people to come forward for prayer or inspire faith to believe for a healing miracle.

Like the example given of the word of wisdom in operation, the gift of the word of knowledge could equally be used in our day-to-day witness. "I was praying for you, and I felt God telling me…" A word of knowledge could unlock an unbeliever's heart to hear the Gospel!

I recall on one occasion being asked to speak on the subject of healing at a special dinner/speaker event outside my local area. After I had shared the message, I invited people to come forward for prayer for healing. As people began to come forward, the Holy Spirit gave me a word of knowledge. I felt the Holy Spirit telling me that among the people coming forward would be a young woman. She would not be able to tell me what was wrong because she had been sexually abused and would be too embarrassed to talk about it.

The Holy Spirit told me to trust Him on what to do next when that young woman came for prayer. I prayed for a number of people, but no young woman. Then, at the end of the prayer session, a young woman came forward, her head down, her shoulders drooping. As I came to pray for her, I quietly said to her, "The Lord has told me about you, and you find it difficult to talk about what is going on in your life. Is that right?"

She nodded and began to cry.

I went on, "You have been hurt by someone in a way that is difficult to talk about."

Again, she nodded and shed more tears.

I then said, "I'm going to pray for you, and I believe the Lord is going to send help before this evening is over." I prayed for her, and as I finished praying, a lady came up to me and said that she wanted to introduce me to her husband.

I was a little annoyed that I had been interrupted because I was still seeking to help the young woman.

The lady then told me that her husband was a local doctor. I began to see how the Lord was working! Whilst the lady went off to get her husband, I asked the young woman whether she would be willing to talk to the doctor and his wife. She agreed to talk to them. The lady came back, saying that her husband would be over in a few minutes. I asked the young woman if we could talk to the doctor's wife. She agreed.

As I introduced her and briefly explained what the problem was, the doctor's wife began to shed some tears. She had gone through a comparable situation herself! I was so amazed at how God, who knows everything, had brought everything together. I was able to leave the young woman with the doctor's wife. I learned (and need to keep re-learning!) how important it is to listen to the promptings of the Holy Spirit.

The third gift in the revelation group is the gift of discerning spirits. We mentioned this gift when we looked at the subject of people being demonised. This gift allows us to look into the spirit realm. It tells us whether something is happening because of evil spirits, angelic spirits, the Holy Spirit or even the human spirit. This gift can protect us from going into a place where there is demonic activity taking place or guide us in ministry, by showing us what is behind a person's behaviour or illness.

Then we come to what I have described as the demonstration gifts. I have previously described how God gives faith by the Holy Spirit. In praying for the sick, I have from time to time felt a special anointing as I have prayed for individuals and known that God, through me, as a channel, is imparting faith to that person for their healing. Of course, it could be argued that was a gift of healing or even miracles. Does it matter? As I said earlier, it is one Holy Spirit who is the source of all the gifts.

The gift of healings is spoken of in the plural. Why? I am not sure but as there are different forms of sickness, then, could it be that there is a gift of healing for each one? What is the difference between gifts of healing and the working of miracles? Again, does it really matter? It is the Holy Spirit that is at work. Miracles tend to be more instantaneous. There is no explanation, other than that God, with whom all things are possible, has intervened. When a missing eye is restored, then that is a miracle!

A lady, in the church that I once pastored in Bristol, told me that she came to Christ in a Stephen Jeffreys (healing evangelist) meeting. She had been sat by a lady who had an empty socket where there should have been an eye. This lady went forward for prayer and as she was being prayed for a new eye was formed! Now, that is a miracle! No wonder, the lady in my church came to Christ. Miracles are not restricted to the human body. The gift of miracles may operate in the miraculous provision of food (Matthew 14:17-21), miraculous interventions with the weather (Mark 4:37-39) and so on.

Many years ago, I had a friend who had been an evangelist in Sri Lanka. At their meetings, it was customary to also feed the people. On one occasion, more people turned up than they had food for. They prayed over their rice and curry. As they served the food, everyone was fed, with food left over.

If miracles are instantaneous, then healings may happen at once or over a period of time. It's as if God, the Holy Spirit, stimulates the body to do what it cannot do of itself and causes a healing recovery. Jesus said, "Lay hands on the sick, and they shall recover" (Mark 16:18). So often, we can get disappointed if we do not see instant healing, so it's important to realise that God may choose to give a healing recovery. It is still supernatural, doing what the body was unable to do of itself.

I trust that in this overview of the gifts of the Holy Spirit, we recognise that we can all be used, not just in a church setting, but in our day-to-day lives. Let us walk in the Spirit, be daily filled with the Spirit and be open to the promptings of the Holy Spirit. The more I sense God's presence in my own life, or the more I sense God's presence in a church meeting, the more I am likely to be used.

Chapter 13
Motivation to Heal the Sick

One of the most moving stories in the New Testament is when a man with a severe case of leprosy comes to Jesus. Imagine his story to that point in time. At some point in his life, he had noticed a sore plus some skin discoloration and numbness to his skin. The Jewish law required him to show himself to a priest for examination. He would have done so, and then been told that he had one of the most dreaded diseases of that time—leprosy.

Such a diagnosis would mean being immediately cut off from his family and society in general. Quarantined to a leprosy colony, his future was not only one of social isolation but of being left to experience a progressive disease, eroding away at his peripheral nerves—a slow agonising death. The only company would be fellow sufferers. For food, they would rely on friends and relatives, from outside the leprosy colony, leaving food for them. If ever they ventured away from the quarantine of the colony, then they had to call out the words, 'Unclean! Unclean!' (Leviticus 13:45). Hopeless, helpless.

When Luke, himself a physician, describes the leper who comes to Jesus, he describes him as a man full of leprosy

(Luke 5:12). In other words, the man's disease was well advanced and quite likely, he has several infected sores hidden under foul smelling rag makeshift bandages, missing digits, weakened limbs, and facial disfigurement. Into this man's world of hopelessness, helplessness, isolation, and suffering, he hears a name that births hope. That name is Jesus! Despite the severity of his condition and the warnings not to move outside the leprosy colony, this man decides to get to where he has heard Jesus is.

It is a huge risk. He might get stoned, or a wild beast might attack him, but he is determined to do it. As he gets to the place, where Jesus is, the crowds around Jesus scream out, "Leper!" Some throw stones at him, but quickly, the crowd disperses, until there are only two people left on the street, Jesus, and the leper. Jesus moves towards the leper and the leper in response, kneels down and worships Jesus, saying:

> Lord if you are willing, You can make me clean. (Luke 5:12)

Mark then writes:

> Then Jesus, moved with compassion, stretched out His hand and touched him, and said to him, "I am willing; be cleansed." As soon as He had spoken, immediately the leprosy left him, and he was cleansed. (Mark 1:41-42)

I love this. Jesus was moved with compassion. In those few moments, Jesus felt the heartache, the loneliness, the hopelessness, the helplessness, the pain, and the suffering of the leper. That is compassion. The Greek word used here is 'splagchnizomai' which literally means, 'to have the bowels yearning'.[29]

We may use the phrase, 'his heart went out to him'. Whatever, Jesus did that which no other person had dared to do for a long time—he touched him. Jesus did not stand away from him, He identified with him, placed His hand on him, and healed him.

On another occasion, Jesus is about to enter the city of Nain. As He does so, a funeral cortege is moving in the opposite direction towards the city cemetery. Following the open-topped coffin is the pathetic figure of an incredibly sad widow lady. Behind her are the professional mourners, wailing and lamenting.

The fact that she was a widow tells us that this lady had already experienced the heartbreak and grief of having buried her husband, and now, her only son was dead. In the society in which she lived, without a son to help her, she faced the prospects of a lonely future, struggling to find the means to stay alive. Grief upon grief. Luke, in recording this event, writes:

> When the Lord saw her, He had compassion on her and said to her, "Do not weep." Then He came and touched the open coffin, and those who carried him stood still. And He said, "Young man, I say to you, arise." So, he was dead sat up and began to speak. And He presented him to his mother. (Luke 7:13-15)

---

[29] Vines Concordance of the Bible.

Once again, Jesus is moved with compassion. His heart goes out to this poor widow lady, feeling her grief and pain. What a joy it must have been to present the son, alive, to his mother.

Matthew's Gospel records:

> Jesus went about all the cities and villages, teaching in their synagogues, preaching the Gospel of the kingdom, and healing every sickness and every disease among the people. But when He saw the multitudes, He was moved with compassion for them, because they were weary and scattered, like sheep having no shepherd. (Matthew 9:35-36)

Compassion was the major motivating factor behind the healing ministry of Jesus. Another Greek word that is used of Jesus and of God is 'agapao'[30]. Love that gives of itself for another.

In the charismatic church at Corinth, things had gotten out of control. Regarding the gifts of the Holy Spirit, people in that church were using so-called utterances of the Holy Spirit for their own purposes and self-advancement. No wonder that Paul, after writing about the gifts of the Spirit and ministries and relationships within the body of Christ, goes on to write the beautiful words of 1 Corinthians 13:

> Though I speak with the tongues of men and of angels, but have not love, I have become sounding brass or a clanging cymbal. And though I have the

---

[30] Vines Concordance of the Bible.

gift of prophecy and understand all mysteries and all knowledge, and though I have all faith, so that I could remove mountains, but have not love, I am nothing. And although I bestow all my good to feed the poor, and though I give my body to be burned, but have not love, it profits me nothing.

Love suffers long and is kind; love does not envy; love does not parade itself, is not puffed up; does not behave rudely, does not seek its own, is not provoked, thinks no evil; does not rejoice in iniquity, but rejoices in the truth; bears all things, believes all things, hopes all things, endures all things.

Love never fails. But whether there are prophecies, they will fail; whether there are tongues, they will cease; whether there is knowledge, it will vanish away. For we know in part, and we prophesy in part. But when that which is perfect has come, then that which is in part will be done away.

When I was a child, I spoke as a child, I understood as a child, I thought as a child; but when I became a man, I put away childish things. For now, we see through a mirror dimly, but then face to face. Now I know in part, but then I shall know just as I also am known. And now abide faith, hope, love, these three; but the greatest of these is love. (1 Corinthians 13:1-13)

Healings, miracles, and utterances are nothing without love. This is no ordinary kind of love; it is the love of God (agapao). The love that gives itself, as in Christ on the cross; the love that is unfailing; the love that loves the unlovely; the love that is consistent and true. A simple test of whether we have that love is to replace the word love with the word 'I' in verses four to seven of the thirteenth chapter of 1 Corinthians. The verses then read like this:

> I suffer long and I am kind; I do not envy; I do not parade myself; I am not puffed up; I do not behave rudely, I do not seek my own, am not provoked, think no evil; I do not rejoice in iniquity, but rejoice in the truth; I bear all things, believe all things, hope all things, endure all things. I do not fail.

This is the love test. I am sure that it makes us all realise how little we have of God's love in our lives. Before we get too discouraged, that love is made available to us by the Holy Spirit.

Paul, in his letter to the Romans, writes of the "love of God poured out into our hearts by the Holy Spirit who was given to us" (Romans 5:5). This love is a fruit of the Holy Spirit (Galatians 5:22). The key, therefore, to experiencing more of this love, is to be filled, refilled, and increasingly filled with the Holy Spirit.

From writing about love, Paul moves on to write about the operation of the gifts of the Spirit, in particular the vocal gifts, tongues, interpretation and prophecy. He writes:

> Pursue love, and desire spiritual gifts. (1 Corinthians 14:1)

Paul is saying, quite clearly that love must be the motivation behind the gifts—and that means all the gifts. Sick and hurting people need to be treated with love and respect. The last thing we need to see are sick people being treated roughly, spoken to coarsely and told such things as it is their unbelief or, worse still, a demonic influence that is causing their sickness—all to make some so-called healing evangelist look good.

Remember, it is God who gives faith and in the event that there are demonic influences causing the sickness, then we should be setting the sick person free! Our prayer needs to be, "Lord Jesus, give me your heart and help me to see people through your eyes."

Good Samaritan story

When a young lawyer asks Jesus, "Teacher, what shall I do to inherit eternal life?"

Jesus asks him, "What is written in the law? What is your reading of it?"

The lawyer replies, "You shall love the Lord your God with all your heart, with all your soul, with all your strength, and with all your mind, and your neighbour as yourself."

The lawyer then asks Jesus, "Who is my neighbour?"

Jesus replies by telling the parable of the Good Samaritan (Luke 10:29-37).

A man, travelling down from Jerusalem to Jericho, is attacked by thieves, robbed, beaten, stripped and left half dead. A priest travels down the same road and when he catches sight of the body of the beaten, half-dead man, fearing for his own safety and not wanting to get ceremonially unclean (through touching a dead body), he passes by on the other side. A Levite (priest's assistant) also travels on the same road, pauses, and looks at the beaten, half-dead man, and then, like the priest, passes by on the other side.

Finally, along comes a Samaritan. When he sees the beaten, half-dead man, he has compassion for him. He thinks to himself, "That could be me. What would I want someone to do for me if I was in that predicament?"

His heart goes out to the unfortunate man. He goes to the man, and bandages his wounds, cleaning and disinfecting them with oil and wine. He puts the man on his own animal, takes him to an inn and cares for him. The next day he pays the innkeeper to look after him, promising to pay any extra costs on his return.

Jesus asks the lawyer, "So which one of the three do you think was neighbour to him who fell among thieves?"

And he said, "He who showed mercy on him."

Then Jesus said to him, "Go and do likewise."

Three philosophies are caught up in this story. The philosophy of the bandits was "What is yours is mine." The philosophy of the priest and Levite was, "What is mine is mine." The philosophy of the Samaritan was, "What is mine is yours."

If we are to love our neighbour as ourselves—and that includes our sick 'neighbour' whoever they may be, then we too need the philosophy of the Samaritan—compassionate hearts that go out to the sick and hurting. The way we would want to be treated—then that is the way we should be treating others.

During times of ministry, it is so important to lovingly talk to a sick person, who has come forwards for prayer, taking time to listen to their need and respond appropriately. Let them be aware that you genuinely love them and that, together with them, you are looking to the Lord to meet their need. If you feel that it is proper to lay hands on them, then ask them first! Whilst there is something special about the power of touch, it will have an adverse effect, if the person does not want to be touched! By touch, I mean a hand on their head or shoulder. Certainly not anywhere inappropriate!

When Jesus was moved with compassion, reached out, and touched the leper that in itself would have been a blessing. To be touched by another human being, after years of quarantine and isolation. Of course, when Jesus touched him, in a moment, in the twinkling of an eye, he was healed! At a basic level, touch, done appropriately, has been shown to be beneficial to an individual's well-being.

In an article entitled, 'The power of touch'[31], Joe Moran, a social and cultural historian writes, "In recent years the caring professions have revived the practice of healing through touch. The tender touch of others is known to boost the immune system, lower blood pressure, decrease the levels of stress hormones such as cortisol and trigger the release of the same kind of opiates as pain-killing drugs. Premature babies gain weight when rubbed lightly from head to foot. Massages reduce pain in pregnant women. People with dementia who are hugged and stroked are less prone to irritability and depression."

As we minister, let love be our motivation, and where proper (and with permission), let us reach out and touch the sick and needy!

---

[31] Joe Moran, The Guardian, Sunday 28th February 2021.

Chapter 14
Authority to Heal the Sick

On one occasion a centurion came to Jesus requesting that Jesus come and heal his servant who was lying at home paralysed and dreadfully tormented. Jesus said to him, "I will come and heal him." What is interesting is what the centurion says next.

> Lord, I am not worthy that You should come under my roof. But only speak a word, and my servant will be healed. For I also am a man under authority, having soldiers under me. And I say to this one, 'Go', and he goes; and to another one, 'Come', and he comes; and to my servant, 'Do this', and he does it.
> When Jesus heard it, He marvelled, and said to those who followed, "Assuredly, I say to you, I have not found such great faith, not even in Israel!" (Matthew 8:5-10)

The centurion was a man under Caesar's authority. Because he was a man under authority, he had the authority to give orders and commands. Submitted to Caesar's authority, he transmitted Caesar's authority. As he watched

Jesus in action, he recognised the same principle at work in Jesus. Jesus was 100% submitted to His Father's authority.

Because He was submitted to His Father's authority, He transmitted His Father's authority. The same principle applies to us. As we submit to Jesus' authority over our lives, then we can transmit His authority. That includes healing the sick.

> He called His twelve disciples together and gave them power and authority over all demons, and to cure diseases. (Luke 9:1)

The Greek word for authority, in relationship to ministry, is exousia (e.g. Matthew 7:29, Luke 4:36). The commonly used Greek word for power is dunamis (e.g. Acts 1:8). We need both! We can call Jesus our Saviour, but to transmit His authority, He must be Lord and Saviour.

All that I am, all that I have and all that I ever hope to be, is His! I am to present myself as living sacrifice (Romans 12:1), dead to self and alive to God. I just become the manager (or steward) of all that I have, managing it on His behalf and at His instruction.

The Apostle Paul, in writing to the Philippians, says:

> Let this mind be in you, which was also in Christ Jesus, who being in the form of God, did not consider it robbery to be equal with God, but made Himself of no reputation, taking the form of a bondservant, and coming in the likeness of men. And being found in appearance as a man, He humbled Himself and became obedient to the point of death, even the death of the cross.

Therefore, God has highly exalted Him and given Him the name above every name, that at the name of Jesus every knee should bow, of those in heaven, and of those on earth, and of those under the earth, and that every tongue should confess that Jesus Christ is Lord, to the glory of God the Father. (Philippians 2:5-11)

We are encouraged to adopt the mind of Jesus in the outworking of His ministry here on earth. This includes humility, servanthood, and obedience. It is from these attributes that spring authority. In practical terms, this is where fasting is so important.

Fasting

On one occasion the disciples had tried casting out a demon and failed. When Jesus arrives, the father of the afflicted boy explains what has been going on. Jesus asks for the boy to be brought to Him. Immediately the demon causes the boy to go into a convulsion. Jesus commands the demon to leave and enter him no more.

Later the disciples ask, "Why could we not cast it out?"

Jesus replies, "This kind can come out by nothing but prayer and fasting" (Mark 9:14-29).

There are several different fasts. There is an absolute fast—no food or water. This fast is inadvisable unless your name is Moses! After just a matter of a few days, you could run into serious health problems. Then there is fasting without food. A healthy, well-nourished male could fast like this for up to forty days.

After that, real hunger (not just the sugar withdrawal hunger of the first few days) sets in, where the body begins to eat away at its own tissue (Matthew 4:2—Jesus). Then there are partial fasts such as missing meals, or just eating small amounts of very basic food. This type of fasting includes what people refer to as the Daniel fast (Daniel 10:2-3, Daniel 1:12).

There are those who would add another category of fasting called a 'soul fast'. This is where a person gives up such things as social media or TV, in order to spend more time seeking God. Those with medical conditions should get advice before fasting from food, but generally speaking, partial fasts, where you are taking some food, should not be an issue.

Whichever type of fasting we choose to engage in, the purpose of the fast is to humble the flesh (Psalm 35:13), to recognise our reliance upon God, and to spend time seeking the face of God. It helps if there is a distinct focus on what we are praying for. As we fast, our praying is intensified, our spirit is enlarged to receive more of the Holy Spirit, and, best of all, we draw closer to God and are in a better position to hear the voice of God. As a result of the fast, we will find ourselves operating at a new level of authority.

For many years, I have tried to fast one day a week. I may have a small dish of bran flakes (which I dislike!) to keep me going, but I don't have the usual meals and don't watch TV programmes (other than catching up with the news). This allows me more time to seek the Lord, and if I can get to additional prayer meetings, I do. To some, this may not seem to be a lot, but I notice the difference when I minister on a Sunday. I feel a greater sense of the anointing of the Holy

Spirit and authority in my speaking. When I have not spent the time fasting—there is not the same edge.

James may well have had fasting in mind when he writes:

> Therefore, submit to God. Resist the Devil and he will flee from you. Draw near to God and He will draw near to you.
> Humble yourselves in the sight of the Lord, and He will lift you up. (James 4:7, 10)

What fasting is not is a form of spiritual weight watchers. In fact, there can be a rebound after fasting, where we gain weight. Neither is fasting meant to be undertaken thinking of the big meal you are going to have when it is over! Fasting is unto the Lord, and He must be the focus. When we are fasting for more than one or two days, then we need to be aware that we are entering an intense spiritual warfare zone (Daniel 10:10-13, Matthew 4:1-3) and need to keep focussed on the Lord, His Word, His name, and the power of His blood.

Timing

Another aspect of authority that we need to consider is timing. As we saw earlier in this book, there are two Greek words for the word of God. One is logos referring to the general word of God, and the other is rama referring to the specific word of God. The same is true for time.

Chronos is the word for time in general and kairos for a definite, specific moment of time. God is sovereign and there are specific moments in time when He chooses to act. For our part, we need to be aware, listening, and obedient to act.

An example of this timing is seen in the healing of the lame man at the Beautiful Gate leading to the temple in Jerusalem. Jesus must have passed this man many times but chose not to heal him because there was a special moment when God would use that man's healing as a mighty evangelistic opportunity. The Day of Pentecost had occurred and already three thousand people had come to Christ and many more were being saved on a daily basis.

Sometime, shortly after, Peter and John are on their way to the temple at the hour of prayer. The lame man had been laid, as was his regular habit, at the Beautiful Gate to ask alms from those going into the temple. Seeing Peter and John, he asks them for alms.

> And fixing his eyes on him, with John, Peter said, "look at us." So, he gave them his attention, expecting to receive something from them. Then Peter said, "Silver and gold I do not have, but what I do have I give you: In the name of Jesus Christ of Nazareth, rise up and walk." And he took him by the right hand and lifted him up, and immediately his feet and ankle bones received strength. So, he, leaping up, stood, and walked and entered the temple with them—walking, leaping, and praising God. And all the people saw him walking and praising God. (Acts 3:4-9)

This was God's moment, God's timing, and in that moment, Peter spoke with authority in the name of Jesus. Faith was imparted to the man, through Jesus's name, and the miracle occurred. The crowds gathered; Peter spoke; and about five thousand men were saved! May we have moments like that—an amazing blend of power, compassion, authority, and timing.

Consider poor Lazarus. He had to die before he was healed! Jesus said to His disciples when news of Lazarus' sickness was brought to Him:

> This sickness in not unto death, but for the glory of God, that the Son of God may be glorified through it. (John 11:4)

Of course, Lazarus did die. His sisters, Mary and Martha were upset when Jesus delayed coming in response to their request. "Lord, if You had been here, my brother would not have died," they each said. God had His timing.

What a mighty miracle took place when Jesus shouted into the opened tomb, "Lazarus, come forth!" Lazarus did, raised from the dead and healed! Yes, the timing was such that Jesus was glorified through the miracle that took place. God being glorified should be the focus of all healings.

It is God's will to heal as much as it is to save the lost. Many times, we have seen people come to church for several weeks, where they hear a clear presentation of the Good News of Jesus, yet they do not respond. Then, one week, sometimes unexpectedly, they respond and give their lives to Jesus, accepting Him as their Lord and Saviour.

So it is with healing. God is sovereign in all things, and that includes the timing of our healing. Be it now, in the near future, or at the trumpet sound, He will heal!

Opportunity

Another aspect of timing is opportunity. If we ask the Lord to give us opportunities, then He will! For our part, we have to be ready to respond to the prompting of the Holy Spirit and take the opportunity. We see such an opportunity unfold in Acts chapter twenty-eight.

> In that region there was an estate of the leading citizen of the island, whose name was Publius, who received us and entertained us courteously for three days. And it happened that the father of Publius lay sick of a fever and dysentery. Paul went into him and prayed, and he laid his hands on him and healed him.
> So, when this was done, the rest of those on the island who had diseases also came and were healed. (Acts 28:7-9)

Paul had just survived a shipwreck, been bitten by a poisonous snake, and survived with no ill effect. He is then invited to the home of Publius. The phrase, 'and it happened' indicates to me that this is a 'kairos' moment, and Paul responds to it. I want us to look carefully at how Paul ministers in this situation, as it is a helpful guide as to how we can minister.

- Step 1. Paul became aware of a need. We can become aware of a need, for example, a sick work colleague or neighbour.
- Step 2. Paul went into him. We visit the sick person or go and talk to the sick person. I am quite sure that Paul introduced himself. They may have passed a few

moments in general conversation, talking about the shipwreck and Paul asking about the illness and expressing how sorry he was that he was sick.

- Step 3. Paul prays for him. After establishing some rapport, Paul would ask if it would be okay to pray for him. In my experience, if we have been courteous and established some rapport, then people rarely refuse prayer. They may say that they do not believe in God, but at that point, I say, "That's okay, I do!" Audible prayer is an immensely powerful way of introducing people to a personal relationship with God. As they hear you talking spontaneously to the Lord in prayer, that is a witness in itself. That said, do not make the prayer into a Gospel sermon!
- Step 4. Paul laid his hands on him. Paul may have told Publius' father that he was going to lay hands on him, on his head or shoulder or taken him by the hand, before he prayed, or as Paul was praying, he felt God's presence, and may have said something like this, "I feel God's presence and, if its okay, I'm going to lay my hands upon you, as I believe God wants to heal you." Whatever Paul did, with the permission of the sick person, we can do the same. We do not have to make any rash claims. We are the channel; God is the Healer! If we sense God's presence, then at the very least (in my experience), the sick person senses the peace and presence of God.
- Step 5. God heals him. It is likely that it was an instantaneous healing, but likewise, it could have been a speedy recovery. Whatever, the man was healed, and word got out. Soon many more sick

people came to where Paul was and were healed. When we pray for someone, we can ask them, "Did you feel God touching you through me?" You may get an instant answer, "Why, yes, and I feel better already!" They may say, "Yes, I felt something." You could reply, "That is great, I will catch up with you in a few days. The Bible says, 'Lay hands on the sick and they will recover'." Whatever the outcome, there will be an opportunity to share more about Jesus and one opportunity could lead to a whole lot more—as in Paul's case!

These five steps are useful guides for Spirit-filled, Christian believers everywhere to minister to their sick neighbours, friends, relatives, and work colleagues. Imagine if we all did that! Imagine the impact we could have—the countless numbers of people who could be introduced to a personal relationship with Jesus through our healing prayers. I could share many opportunities that I have had, but for now, I will share just one.

Recently, I had to get my front tyres checked on my car. They need replacing. As I was waiting in the tyre waiting room, an employee came in with his manager. The employee was in severe pain. The day before he had been involved in a road traffic collision and had injured his back.

Because the pain had intensified, his manager had phoned for an ambulance to take him to hospital. As I was the only other person in the waiting room, I could not but help get involved in their conversation. I joined in. I told them that I was a recently retired doctor and asked a few medical-type questions. I then asked if it would be okay to do a brief examination.

I did this. By now, there was a rapport established. I then felt the prompting of the Holy Spirit, "Why don't you pray for him?" I said to the employee (by now, I knew his name), "This may sound strange to you, but as well as being a doctor, I am a Christian minister. If it is okay with you, I would like to pray for you. I do not know if you believe in prayer and that kind of thing?"

He replied, "Not really, but I'll give anything a go right now."

I said, "That's okay, I believe in the power of prayer and as I pray for you, I'm going to place a hand on your shoulder." I prayed, audibly, for him. I handed him and his manager an invitation card to a carol concert at a church that I had attended the previous week. At that point, I was told my car was ready.

A few days later I was passing the tyre place and decided to call in and check up on the employee. The manager was not there, and the employee was on a few days leave, expected back at the beginning of the following week. The person at the desk knew all about what had gone on! He said that the employee had gone to the hospital, been checked over, told there was nothing serious going on and advised to have a couple of days rest! 'Lay hands on the sick and they shall recover'. I look forward to the next opportunity I have when my tyres need attending to! Any situation can become a God opportunity.

Chapter 15
Suffering

I had been asked to take part in a programme for Radio Merseyside. I was told to take along some of my favourite Christian music, and the plan was that, between tracts, I would answer some questions about my Christian faith. I readily accepted the opportunity, thinking that it should not be too difficult. I had assumed that the Christian minister who had contacted me would be doing the interviewing. How wrong I was!

When I arrived, I was told that the person who would be interviewing me was not a Christian and had a reputation for being a challenging interviewer. After introducing me and playing one of the first pieces of music, he said, "I would like to hear your views on the reason for suffering in the world. Last week I interviewed a clergyman from Liverpool Cathedral, and he was unable to give me an answer." I responded, "There is no quick answer to explain the reason for suffering in the world, but what I can say is this, God understands suffering."

He said, "What do you mean, God understands suffering."

I replied, "God in Jesus was falsely tried, beaten beyond recognition, and then subjected to death by crucifixion—a cruel, painful, agonising death. There is more I could say, but God understands suffering, having suffered, and is able to come alongside those who suffer and help them in their suffering."

He nodded and said, "Thank you," and moved on to the next piece of music.

Answers have to be short and snappy in that kind of radio format, but if I had had time, I could have spoken of how Christ's suffering began before his arrest and crucifixion. In Gethsemane, Mark records Jesus saying to Peter, James, and John, "My soul is exceedingly sorrowful, even to death" (Mark 14:34). Luke, in his Gospel, adds:

> And being in agony, He prayed more earnestly. Then His sweat became like great drops of blood falling down to the ground. (Luke 22:44)

If we were asked, "What was Christ's greatest agony?" then it's likely that we would reply that it was His being nailed to and hung from the cross, or possibly the agony he experienced at the whipping post when Roman soldiers took it in turn to lash his back with a multi-stranded whip, each strand tipped with a piece of metal. There is no doubting the physical agony of either the cross or the whipping post, but Gethsemane is quite possibly where Christ experienced His greatest agony. This is suffering and agony that we will never fully understand—the pure, spotless, sinless Son of God surrendering Himself to the Father's will, being prepared to go to the cross, and take upon Himself the sin of the world, thus becoming the sacrificial sin offering for all of us.

For a moment, think of a lady (in olden times) brought up in some posh mansion, where she has lived a sheltered life, always being spoken to, and treated with the utmost respect. Take that same lady and thrust her into some seedy, smoke-filled tavern, filled with drunken, drug-crazed, individuals who begin to address her with foul language, molest her and crudely treat her. Imagine the horror and the repulsion she would feel. Multiply that a million times and more, and, just maybe, we begin to get the slightest insight into what Jesus was experiencing.

No wonder that Luke, the doctor, notes that Jesus began to sweat, as it were, great drops of blood. The intensity of what Jesus was going through not only made him sweat profusely, but the strain caused blood vessels supplying his sweat glands to burst—thus it appeared He was sweating great drops of blood. What suffering!

Of course, Jesus showed that He identifies with us in our humanity and our suffering even before Gethsemane and Calvary. When God chose to step into this world of ours, He did so in a way we could all understand. Using the womb of the virgin Mary as His channel, He comes as a baby. His birthplace was not some princely palace or priestly temple but the filth and squalor of a stable. Wrapped in bits of cloth, He is laid in a manger—an animal feeding trough.

The poorest of the poor can identify with that. Before the age of two, he was a refugee, fleeing from King Herod. His earliest years were spent growing up in some foreign land before the family moved back to Nazareth. Mary and Joseph went on to have other children—at least four boys and two girls (Mark 6:3).

If, as assumed, Joseph died, then for a time Jesus would have become the breadwinner for this sizeable family. During His ministry, despite being a blessing to many, rejection and false accusations followed Him wherever He went. Isaiah prophesied of Jesus suffering:

> He is despised and rejected by men, a Man of sorrows and acquainted with grief. And we hid, as it were, our faces from Him; He was despised, and we did not esteem Him. Surely, He has born our griefs and carried our sorrows; yet we esteemed Him stricken, smitten by God, and afflicted, but He was wounded for our transgressions, He was bruised for our iniquities; the chastisement of our peace was upon Him. And by His stripes we are healed.
> All we like sheep have gone astray; we have turned, everyone, to his own way; and the Lord has laid on Him the iniquity of us all. (Isaiah 53:3-6)

Note that, 'He was despised and rejected by men, a Man of sorrows and acquainted with grief'. It's not just physical suffering that Jesus endured but also real, deep emotional suffering.

We could continue to analyse the life and ministry of Jesus, but I trust from what we have said so far:

> Seeing then that we have a great high priest who has passed through the heavens, Jesus the Son of God, let us hold fast our confession. For we do not have a high priest who cannot sympathise with our weaknesses, but was in all points tempted as we are, yet without

sin. Let us therefore come boldly to the throne of grace, that we may obtain mercy and find grace to help in time of need. (Hebrews 4:14-16)

We see this high priest in action at the cross. Not only does Jesus, in the midst of his own suffering, have time for a dying thief, but also for his mother. Mary is stood at the foot of the cross. She must have been experiencing so many different emotions. Heartache, confusion, helplessness, and anger at the baying crowds. So many questions, but seemingly no answers.

With the benefit of knowing what happens next, we could say, "It's okay Mary. It will be so different in three days' time." But for someone living in that awful dark moment, three days is an extremely long time. Jesus, our great high priest, knows that. He sees Mary. He sees the turmoil she is going through.

> When Jesus therefore saw His mother, and the disciple whom He loved standing by, He said to His mother, "Woman behold your son!" Then He said to the disciple, "Behold your mother!" And from that hour that disciple took her to his own home. (John 19:26-27)

In His own suffering, Jesus ministers to his suffering mother and ensures that she is cared for. What a Saviour! What a lesson to us. So often, when we suffer, we want to hold a pity party. The example of Jesus is in suffering minister to others who are suffering.

What a comfort to know that Jesus is my high priest. He understands me, my emotional pain, and my physical pain, He knows what I am going through, and He is praying for me and will give me the grace to go through it. The last book of the Bible is a great illustration of this.

Revelation: a book of comfort

At the time that John received the revelation that is the Book of Revelation, it was not an easy time to be a Christian. Christians were seen as a threat to Caesar. False accusations, arrests, confiscation of property, imprisonment and summary executions, including facing gladiators and wild animals in the Roman arenas, were all part of the challenges facing committed Christians. Dark and tough times where suffering was never far away. John himself was a prisoner on the Isle of Patmos.

Forced to quarry stone for the Romans, life could not have been easy on that island, especially for a man, who by then, was quite elderly. Despite that, John maintains his walk with God. During one of his times of prayer and communion with God, his prayer life goes to a whole new level. He receives an amazing revelation which he is able to record and then pass on to the church. Many people struggle with the Book of Revelation, and sure, it has things in it which are difficult to understand but think of how those early Christians would have been encouraged by it.

It begins with a Revelation of Jesus, the righteous judge, who is one with His church, feeling for His church and encouraging His church. There's encouragement, correction and then more encouragement, followed by a promise of a reward to those who overcome (note to leaders—what a great lesson in people management!). Then, there is a glimpse of heaven and worship around the throne of God. It continues by showing there will be a time of darkness and tribulation, but these very works of darkness and evil in the world are going to be judged.

God is going to pour out His wrath upon them and then, Jesus is coming again, as King of Kings and Lord of Lords. He will set up His rule upon the earth. Following the final judgement of Satan and of all those whose names are not written in the Lamb's book of life, God will usher in a new heaven and a new earth where Jesus, the Lamb, will reign forever and ever. The Lamb wins!

That may seem a simple overview of the Book of Revelation but think of how it would have encouraged those Christians, alive at the time it was written. I can hear them saying, "We are going through difficult trials and persecution, but the Lord is not going to let it go unpunished. Jesus is with us. He is coming again, and whatever happens, we are going to be with Him for ever and ever."

Along with John, Paul wrote to Christians suffering persecution. In Romans chapter eight, a chapter that begins with 'no condemnation' and ends with 'no separation', Paul writes:

> For you did not receive the spirit of bondage again to fear, but you received the Spirit of adoption by whom we cry out, "Abba, Father." The Spirit Himself bears witness with our spirit that we are children of God, and if children, then heirs—heirs of God and joint

heirs with Christ, if indeed we suffer with Him, that we may also be glorified together.

Who shall separate us from the love of Christ? Shall tribulation, or distress, or persecution, or famine, or nakedness, or peril, or sword? As it is written:

For Your sake we are killed all day long; we are accounted as sheep for the slaughter.

Yet in all these things we are more than conquerors through Him who loved us. For I am persuaded that neither death nor life, nor angels nor principalities nor powers, nor things present not things to come, nor height nor depth, nor any other created thing, shall be able to separate us from the love of God which is in Christ Jesus our Lord. (Romans 8:15-17, 35-39)

Today, in the west, in particular, we get upset by any slight discomfort, whether it be physical, mental, or material. We would moan less if we stopped and, instead, prayed for those who are suffering persecution for their faith in other parts of the world, where there is hostility to the Christian message. As well as that, it would help us if we spent more time focussing on eternal things. This life is transient, but the life ahead of us is eternal!

Job

The book of Job is thought to have been written around the time of the patriarchs (Abraham, Isaac, Jacob), around 2000 years BC. Whenever it was written, it certainly gives us some insights into the age-long problem of human suffering. As well as giving us some human responses to suffering, the book of Job takes us 'behind the scenes' into dark spiritual forces at work causing suffering and concludes by powerfully reminding us that God is sovereign and has the final say, and for Job, his end was to be better than his beginning.

As we begin the book, we find Job is one of the greatest men living in the east at that time. He is a man of prosperity, a man of prayer and a man protected by God. Successful in his business as a farmer, he rises early every morning to pray for his family. At this point in the book, we may feel that Job lives in a different world to us, but everything is about to change. Suddenly, a sequence of tragedies strikes Job.

He loses his oxen, donkeys, sheep, camels, and servants, either through bandit raids or through natural disasters. The final tragedy in this sequence is when a hurricane causes the house where Job's children are gathered, to collapse. Job's children all die in the process. Stripped of his possessions, his farming business in ruins, and bereaved of his children, the Bible says:

> The Job arose, tore his robe, and shaved his head; and he fell to the ground and worshipped. And he said, "Naked I came from my mother's womb, and naked shall I return there. The Lord gave, and the Lord has taken away; blessed be the name of the Lord."
> In all this Job did not sin nor charge God with wrong. (Job 1:20-22)

What a response! In the midst of tragedy, disaster and bereavement, Job worships. He recognised that whereas circumstances change, God cannot change. We may be perplexed and cast down, but He remains faithful, He is God.

In my first pastorate, Pontllanfraith, South Wales, I was privileged to pastor an amazing group of people. One of them was a lady called Anne. She was only forty-nine years old when she died, as a result of cancer. Just fifteen months before she herself died; her husband had suddenly died from a heart attack. John and Anne had been devoted to each other.

Through the last months of her own life, much of it spent in intense pain and suffering, worship dominated her life. She developed a closeness and depth of relationship with God that made many of us, who visited her, feel as though we had only touched the periphery of what it was to know God. She ministered to us. To Anne, healing was only a temporary thing anyway, but knowing God, and getting close to Him, was an eternal reality. This was triumphant faith in action in the face of adversity.

Behind the scenes

The first chapter of Job, as well as introducing Job and telling us of the various tragedies that struck him, also gives us some behind-the-scenes information of what is happening in the spiritual realm. The New Living Translation of the Bible records it like this:

> One day members of the heavenly court came to present themselves before the Lord, and the accuser, Satan came with them. "Where have you come from?" the Lord asked Satan. Satan answered, "I have been patrolling the earth, watching everything that's going on."

Then the Lord asked Satan, "Have you noticed my servant, Job. He is blameless—a man of complete integrity. He fears God and stays away from evil."
Satan replied to the Lord, "Yes, but Job has good reason to fear God. You have always put a wall of protection around him and his home and his property. You have made him prosper in everything he does. Look how rich he is! But reach out and take away everything he has, and he will surely curse you to your face!"
"All right, you may test him," the Lord said to Satan. "Do whatever you want with everything he possesses, but don't harm him physically." So, Satan left the Lord's presence. (Job 1:6-12 NLT)

Satan wasted no time in bringing about the disasters and tragedies about which we have already written. When Job responded in the way in which he did, Satan was furious. Chapter two tells how, once again Satan appears before God. God reminds Satan, that despite the tragedies Job had experienced, he retained his integrity. Satan replies:

> Skin for skin! Yes, all that a man has he will give for his life. But stretch out Your hand now, and touch his bone and his flesh, and he will surely curse you to Your face!
> And the Lord said to Satan, "Behold, he is in your hand, but spare his life." (Job 2:4-6)

At this point, Satan strikes Job with boils all over his body. Many of us have experienced what it is like to have one boil—the pain, the anguish, and the sickly feeling it caused. We can remember how we guarded it, making sure that nothing or no one touched it or came near it. Job was covered in boils! He must have been in intense pain, feverish, nauseated, weak and unable to find rest in any position. At a time when he needed the help and companionship of his wife, more than ever, she only added to his suffering by saying, "Curse God and die!" (Job 2:9). Again, in Job's reply, he maintains his integrity:

> "You speak as one of the foolish women speaks. Shall we indeed accept good from God, and shall we not accept adversity?" In all this Job did not sin with his lips. (Job 2:10)

In these 'behind the scenes' encounters, between Satan and God, not only does God esteem Job, but has every confidence that Job will remain faithful through this time of extreme testing. What is more, God who is above time knows the end from the beginning—something we get to see in the last chapter of Job. God sets the parameters, but Satan wastes no time in attacking Job to the very edge of those parameters. It has been that way since the fall of Adam in the Garden of Eden. Satan is the thief who has come to kill, steal, and destroy (John 10:10a).

Whether it is spoiling creation, attacking man (created in the image of God), marriage and family life, Israel or the church, Satan will try to harm as much as he can—or as much as he is allowed to. Behind wars and conflicts there are spiritual forces at work (e.g. Daniel 10:13). Before we start pointing fingers at God, we need to recognise who the real destroyer is. Thank God for Jesus who has come to give life and life more abundantly (John 10:10b).

Job's friends

Back to Job and most of the rest of the book is taking up with the dialogue between Job and his 'friends'. As someone once pointed out, "If you have friends like Job's, you don't need enemies!"

Those of his friends, the first to speak, express the philosophy, "Job, this has come upon you because you have sinned. This is why you are sick; this is why disaster has struck you. Repent!" As well as everything else, Job has a guilt complex thrust upon him—a complex he resists. However, even Job begins to flag under this constant barrage.

> My spirit is broken, my days are extinguished, the grave is ready for me. (Job 17:1)

Is there any place for this philosophy in explaining sickness and suffering? Yes, if a person is persisting in a sinful lifestyle. If a person gets a sexually transmitted disease because of promiscuity, then their sickness can be explained by their sin. If someone holds bitterness, jealousy, or resentment in their hearts towards another person and subsequently develops physical symptoms such as chest pain or headaches or illnesses such as peptic ulcers or worsening arthritis, then it is not difficult to recognise the relationship between their sin and their sickness.

Only repentance and unconditional forgiveness can put that sick individual on the road to healing. To make a blanket statement that sickness is the result of sin in the life of an individual is not true in the majority of cases. It certainly was not true for Job. There are times when bad things happen to good people.

Consider, Jesus and His disciples, in a boat, crossing the Sea of Galilee (Mark 4:35-41). A severe storm hits them. So severe that experienced fishermen disciples get scared. Yet, you can't be more in the will of God than being in a boat with Jesus, going somewhere at His instruction!

Yes, there was a storm, but Jesus is at peace in the storm and is able to speak peace to the storm. He can do the same in our storms. As we read on, He does that for Job.

Once the older of Job's friends had finished giving their views, the youngest friend shared his philosophy. He, in summary, said, "Job, God is using this time of suffering to teach you a lesson. He wants to refine you." This view may appeal to the ascetic-minded person, but it is not compatible with God, who is our Father in heaven.

God does not inflict sickness on his children in order to teach them lessons! Yes, there can be times when God tests us, but the outcome is always positive with the resultant strengthening of our faith.

> The genuineness of your faith, being much more precious than gold that perishes, though it be tested by fire, may be found to praise, honour, and glory at the revelation of Jesus Christ, who having not seen you love. Though now you do not see Him, yet believing, you rejoice with joy inexpressible and full of glory, receiving the end of your faith—the salvation of your souls. (1 Peter 1:7-9)

What I love in the book of Job is when the darkness cannot get any darker and when hopelessness and despair are at their worst, Job gets a revelation from heaven. For a moment, he is transported two thousand years forward in time and gets a glimpse of Jesus. Note Job's words:

> Oh, that my words were written! Oh, that they were inscribed in a book! That they were engraved on a rock with an iron pen and lead forever!
> For I know that my Redeemer lives, and He shall stand at last on the earth; and after my skin is destroyed, this I know, that in my flesh I shall see God, whom I shall see for myself, and my eyes shall behold, and not another. How my heart yearns within me! (Job 19:23-27)

One of the names attributed to Jesus is that He is 'the lily of the valley' (Song of Solomon 2:1). In the midst of the dark and gloom of a valley experience, He can be found as a beautiful, bright, shining lily. The psalmist said, "Yea, though I walk through the valley of the shadow of death, I will fear no evil; for You are with me" (Psalm 23:4).

We are not exempt from valleys, but He has promised to walk with us in the valley. The first Christian martyr, Stephen, saw heaven opened and Jesus standing at the right hand of God, just before the hostile crowd began to stone him (Acts 7:56). That must have been such a help to Stephen—to focus on Jesus as he came to the end of his own race.

Chapter 16
Ultimate Healing

At the very heart of the Christian message is the bodily resurrection of our Lord Jesus Christ. Because Jesus lives, we shall live! In his first letter to the Corinthians, chapter fifteen, the Apostle Paul, masterfully sets out the case for the resurrection of Jesus. His first appeal is to the Scriptures.

> Christ died for our sins according to the Scriptures, and that He was buried, and that He rose again the third day according to the Scriptures. (1 Corinthians 15:3-4)

Jesus died according to the Scriptures. Paul, no doubt, had in mind Scriptures like Psalm 22 and Isaiah 53. Psalm 22 gives a prophetically inspired, graphic description of someone being crucified. Isaiah 53 prophesies of Christ's substitutionary atoning death (particularly verses 5-6). To those Scriptures, we could add the shadows and types found in the Passover and the offerings at the Tabernacle in the Wilderness.

In the celebration of the Passover, no bone of the sacrificial lamb was to be broken (Exodus 12:46). Because the day following the crucifixion of Jesus was the Sabbath, the Jews had asked Pilate to break the legs of those crucified, in order to speed up their deaths (those undergoing crucifixion needed to push up with their legs to breath. With their legs broken, they would very quickly suffocate to death).

Their bodies could then be taken down before the start of the Sabbath. However, when the soldiers, instructed to do this, came to Jesus, they found that He was already dead. To make absolutely sure, one of the soldiers stuck a spear into Jesus's side, up under his ribs, and into His heart. John, in his Gospel, records it like this:

> But one of the soldiers pierced His side with a spear, and immediately blood and water came out. And he who has seen has testified, and his testimony is true; and he knows that he is telling the truth, so that you may believe. For these things were done that the Scripture should be fulfilled, "Not one of His bones shall be broken." And again, another Scripture says, "They shall look on Him whom they pierced." (Zechariah 12:10; John 19:34-37)

Is there an explanation for the blood and water? I believe so. Death could never take Jesus. He had to allow Himself to die. Following His final cries from the cross, "It is finished" and "Father into Your hands I commit My spirit," Jesus allowed His heart/His myocardium to break.

Blood rapidly filled the pericardial sac (medically we call this, cardiac tamponade), and death very quickly followed. Post-mortem, this blood is divided into a thick cellular layer and a watery serum layer—hence blood and water. This is amazing. Cause of death—a broken heart. Broken for lost humanity.

Jesus was buried according to the Scriptures. As far as the Romans were concerned, a person condemned to die by crucifixion was a non-person. Their bodies were often just thrown onto a rubbish tip or into a communal pit.[32] Not so Jesus. Isaiah prophesied:

> And they shall make His grave with the wicked—but with the rich at His death because He has done no violence, nor was any deceit in His mouth. (Isaiah 53:9)

Joseph of Arimathea, a secret disciple of Jesus and a man of some wealth, asks Pilate, the Roman governor, for the body of Jesus. After binding the body in strips of linen, together with myrrh and aloes, Joseph and Nicodemus lay the body of Jesus in an unused tomb, in a garden close to the place where Jesus had been crucified. To add extra weight to Jesus' burial, the chief priests and Pharisees requested Pilate that the stone at the entrance of the tomb be sealed and that soldiers be placed on guard (Matthew 27:62-65).

Jesus rose again according to the Scriptures. Peter, in addressing the crowd on the Day of Pentecost, refers to the Psalmist David, who prophesied:

> Therefore, my heart is glad, and my glory rejoices; My flesh also will rest in hope. For You will not leave

---

[32] Jewish historian Josephus and others (internet search, "What happened to bodies after crucifixion").

> My soul in Sheol, nor will You allow Your Holy One to see corruption. You will show me the path of life; in Your presence is fullness of joy; at Your right hand are pleasures for evermore. (Psalm 16:8-11, Acts 2:25-28)

God raised Jesus from the dead, a mighty, triumphant, bodily resurrection. The grave clothes could not bind Him, the tomb could not hold Him, the soldiers could not stop Him—up from the grave He arose! Death was defeated!

God

When Job's friends have finished expressing their views, then God Himself speaks to Job. God reveals His infinite greatness, omnipresence, and omniscience. In the face of such a revelation of the Divine Person, Job realises his own utter smallness and insignificance. Job says:

> I know that you can do everything, and that no purpose of Yours can be withheld from You. You asked, "Who is this who hides counsel without knowledge?" Therefore, I have uttered what I did not understand, things too wonderful for me, which I did not know. Listen, please, and let me speak; You said, "I will question you, and you shall answer me." I have now heard of You by the hearing of the ear, but now my eye sees you. Therefore, I abhor myself, and repent in dust and ashes. (Job 42:1-6)

It is, as Job begins to take his eyes off himself and off his circumstances and fixes them upon God that God begins to move in the life of Job. Once Job has prayed for his friends, then God restores Job's losses, in fact, He gives Job twice as much as what he had before. The book that began with Job worshipping, ends with Job worshipping.

Whilst it is understandably easy, in our sickness and suffering, to focus on ourselves and bemoan our situation, complaining that life is not fair, the last part of the book of Job, reminds us to reset our focus. Before the eternal, all-powerful, ever-present God, our life is but a vapour. We need to set our focus on Him. We need to focus on the Healer, rather than the healing, the Blesser rather than the blessings, the Giver rather than the gifts. When all is said and done, He is the potter, and we are the clay ((Isaiah 64:8).

As I close this chapter on suffering, a word to pastors and leaders—it's time to strengthen our theology on suffering. If we were asked what makes Christianity so different to any other world religion, we would say such things as, 'God became flesh and dwelt among us', 'The bodily resurrection of Jesus', 'God's abundant grace', 'We can have a relationship with God and call Him Father'. One area that we can overlook is that Christianity addresses the subject of suffering.

In Buddhism, suffering is to be avoided at all costs. Hinduism sees suffering as 'karmic retribution'—punishment for bad deeds in a previous incarnation. Islam is fatalistic and says it is God's will, and for God to come to earth and suffer is inconceivable.[33] Thank God we have a message that includes suffering, and we have a Saviour who understands our suffering, is able to minister to us in our suffering, and offers us a future free from suffering.

Witnesses

Having appealed to Scriptural evidence, Paul goes on to appeal to the evidence of witnesses.

> He was seen by Cephas, then by the twelve. After that He was seen by over five hundred brethren at once, of whom the greater part remain to the present, but some have fallen asleep. After that He was seen by James, then by all the apostles. Then last of all He was seen by me also, as one born out of due time. (1 Corinthians 15:5-8)

The Gospel writers add to Paul's list. In fact, they tell us that the first witnesses of the risen Jesus are women. Paul may have omitted the women because, in first-century Judea, women were not considered reliable witnesses, and their evidence was not admissible in court.[34] The fact that the Gospel writers include them, tells us that as far as God is concerned, the witness of women is as effective as that of men! Matthew's account tells us that on the first day of the week, Mary Magdalene and the other Mary came to see the tomb. There is an earthquake, as an angel of the Lord

---

[33] Amy Orr Ewing, Where Is God in All the Suffering, The Good Book Company, pages 14 and 102.
[34] Jewish historian Josephus.

descends from heaven, rolls back the stone, and sits on it. The angel says:

> Do not be afraid, for I know that you seek Jesus who was crucified. He is not here, for He is risen, as He said. Come, see the place where the Lord lay. And go quickly and tell His disciples that He is risen from the dead, and indeed He is going before you into Galilee; there you will see Him. Behold, I have told you.
> So they went out quickly form the tomb with fear and great joy and ran to bring His disciples word. And as they went to tell His disciples, Jesus met them, saying, "Rejoice!" So they came and held Him by the feet and worshipped Him. Then Jesus said to them, "Do not be afraid. Go and tell My brethren to go to Galilee, and there they will see Me." (Matthew 28:5-10)

Note that Jesus used the word, "Rejoice." The Greek word—chairete—"Rejoice, we have conquered!" Note how they held Him by the feet.

John in his Gospel concentrates on Mary Magdalene. She had come early, whilst it was still dark, to the tomb, and saw that the stone had been taken from the tomb. She runs and reports this to Peter and John, who then runs to the tomb. Peter goes in and notes the handkerchief that had been around Jesus' head, not lying with the linen clothes, but folded together in a place by itself. It is then that they begin to accept that Jesus is indeed risen from the dead.

They leave, and Mary is left on her own at the tomb. Perplexed, confused and fearful. This is where, in John's account she sees two angels, one at the head and the other at the feet, where the body of Jesus had lain. The angels ask her, "Woman, why are you weeping?"

She replies, "Because they have taken away my Lord, and I do not know where they have laid Him."

> Now when she had said this, she turned around and saw Jesus standing there, and did not know that it was Jesus. Jesus said to her, "Woman, why are you weeping? Whom are you seeking?"
> She, supposing Him to be the gardener, said to Him, "Sir, if you have carried Him away, tell me where you have laid Him, and I will take Him away."
> Jesus said to her, "Mary!" She turned and said to Him, "Rabboni!" (which is to say, Teacher). Jesus said to her, "Do not cling to Me, for I have not yet ascended to My Father; but go to My brethren and say to them, 'I am ascending to My Father and Your Father, and to my God and your God'." (John 20:14-18)

Note how Mary does the very natural thing, and hugs Jesus—'do not cling to me'. You can't hug a spirit!

Mary is the first of three people that Scripture records that Jesus called by name, following His resurrection. The other two are Thomas (who doubted) and Peter (who denied Him). Jesus, the Great Shepherd (Hebrews 13:20), risen from the dead, tends to, speaks to, and restores His hurting sheep.

John continues the resurrection narrative by telling us that, on the same evening, the first day of the week, Jesus comes and stands in the midst of His disciples. He greets them with the words, "Peace be with you." He then shows them His hands and His side. Having done that, He commissions them. Thomas misses that meeting and famously says:

> Unless I see in His hands the print of the nails, and put my finger into His side, I will not believe.
> And after eight days His disciples were again inside, and Thomas with them. Jesus came, the doors being shut, and stood in their midst, and said, "Peace to you!" Then He said to Thomas, "Reach your finger here, and look at My hands; and reach your hand here and put it into My side. Do not be unbelieving but believing."
> And Thomas answered and said to Him, "My Lord and my God!" Jesus said to him, "Thomas because you have seen Me, you have believed. Blessed are those who have not seen me and yet believed." (John 20:25-29)

John concluded his resurrection appearances of Jesus by the side of the Sea of Galilee. Peter and some of the disciples have gone fishing. They fish all night but do not catch a thing. The next morning, Jesus is standing on the shore.

He asks, "Children, have you any food?" They answer, "No." Jesus tells them to cast their net on the other side of the boat. They do and immediately have a large catch of fish. John recognises that it is Jesus, and Peter, rather than wait, dives into the water and swims to the shore. When they arrive at the shore, there is a fire of coals, fish cooking, and bread. Breakfast provided by Jesus!

It is after breakfast that Jesus takes Peter to one side and three times (the same as the number of denials) asks Peter if he loves Him. A restored Peter is recommissioned.

Luke adds one further story to these resurrection appearances found in the Gospels. He writes of the account of two men walking from Jerusalem to Emmaus. Their conversation was taken up with the events of the previous few days. Jesus joins them.

At that point, they do not recognise that it is Jesus. He asks them why they are sad and what is their conversation all about. They are amazed that He has not heard about what had happened! So they tell Him about the events and that certain women had discovered the empty tomb and seen a vision of angels, who stated that Jesus was alive. Jesus says to them:

> O foolish ones, and slow of heart to believe in all the prophets have spoken! Ought not the Christ to have suffered these things and to enter into His glory?
> And beginning at Moses and all the prophets, He expounded to them in all the Scriptures the things concerning Himself. (Luke 24:25-27)

How amazing is that! A Bible study by Jesus, on Jesus. Later, these disciples were to say, "Did not our heart burn within us whilst He talked with us on the road, and whilst He opened the Scriptures." We need a revival of preaching that causes that kind of heartburn!

At the end of their journey, they invite Jesus to come and stay with them. As Jesus takes bread, breaks it and gives it to them, their eyes were opened, and they recognised Him. Jesus disappeared, and despite the lateness of the hour, they returned to Jerusalem, found the eleven, and told them everything that had happened.

> The Lord is risen indeed and has appeared to Simon! (Luke 24:34)

As they were sharing these things, Jesus Himself showed up. After greeting them with the words, "Peace to you," Jesus went on to say:

> Behold My hands and My feet, that it is Myself. Handle Me and see, for a spirit does not have flesh and bones as you see I have. (Luke 24:39)

Paul, in 1 Corinthians 15, adds that He was seen by over five hundred brethren at once. With those we have already mentioned, it adds up to an abundance of witnesses to the bodily resurrection of Jesus. He was recognisable and touchable. He could walk and talk. He could eat food and cook food. As Jesus Himself said, "A spirit does not have flesh and bones as you see me have." Paul does not leave it there. He says:

> Then last of all He was seen by me also, as by one born out of due time. (1 Corinthians 15:8)

To me, this ranks as one of the greatest proofs of the resurrection of Jesus. Paul (or Saul as he was, pre-conversion) was, in his unconverted state, doing all he could to try and snuff out the infant church, arresting, torturing, and even killing believers in Jesus. The harder he tried, the more the church grew! If he was trying to get them to confess to where the body of Jesus was, there was no confession, other than, "Jesus is risen." Knowing that there were believers in Jesus in Damascus, Saul made his way there, with papers allowing him to arrest the believers and take them to Jerusalem. It is on the Damascus road that Saul, himself, meets the risen Jesus.

> As he journeyed, he came near Damascus, and suddenly a light shone around him from heaven. Then he fell to the ground, and heard a voice saying to him, "Saul, Saul, why are you persecuting Me?" And he said, "Who are You, Lord?" Then the Lord said, "I am Jesus, whom you are persecuting. It is hard for you to kick against the goads."
> So he, trembling and astonished, said, "Lord, what do You want me to do?" Then the Lord said to him, "Arise and go into the city, and you will be told what you must do." (Acts 9:3-6)

This experience dramatically changed Saul's life. Saul the destroyer becomes Paul the builder. The greatest opponent becomes the greatest proponent of the resurrection of Jesus and the good news of salvation.

First fruits

How does the resurrection of Jesus affect us? Well, because Jesus lives, we live! Paul writes:

> But now Christ is risen from the dead and has become the first fruits of those who have fallen asleep. For

> since by man came death, by Man also came the resurrection of the dead. For as in Adam all die, even so in Christ all shall be made alive. (1 Corinthians 15:20-22)

The phrase 'first fruits' is referring to a Jewish harvest festival. The feast of first fruits was one of the mandatory Jewish festivals that Jewish adult men had to attend (the others being the feast of Passover and the feast of Ingathering—Exodus 34:22-23. Each of these feasts is a shadow/type of what is to come in the New Testament). At the feast of the first fruits, the children of Israel presented the first fruits of their harvest to the Lord (Leviticus 23:10-11).

This wave offering was in anticipation of the great harvest to follow. Jesus is our first fruits offered to the Father. Now, there is a great harvest to follow. Because of His resurrection, one day we shall be raised!

Paul proceeds to write about the kind of body our resurrection body will be. He refers to both the natural realm and the realm of astronomy. In the natural realm, he writes about seeds. It is sown as grain into the ground but then emerges as a plant. He then writes about the difference in glory between terrestrial bodies and celestial bodies. The point he is making is that, yes, the resurrection body is a very real body, but it has been changed and transformed.

> So also, is the resurrection of the dead. The body is sown in corruption, it is raised in incorruption. It is sown in dishonour; it is raised in glory. It is sown in weakness; it is raised in power. It is sown a natural body; it is raised a spiritual body. (1 Corinthians 15:42-44)

This great chapter concludes with the words:

> Behold, I tell you a mystery: We shall not all sleep, but we shall all be changed—in a moment, in the twinkling of an eye, at the last trumpet. For the trumpet will sound, and the dead will be raised incorruptible, and we shall be changed. For this corruptible must put on incorruption, and this mortal must put on immortality.
>
> Thanks be to God, who gives us the victory through our Lord Jesus Christ. (1 Corinthians 15:51-53,57)

This is the ultimate healing! Corruptible—pain-filled, disease-stricken, mortal bodies, changed and transformed into pain-free, sickness-free, incorruptible, immortal, resurrection bodies.

When we die

At death, the soul (that part of us that gives us individuality and personality, which includes our conscience and will) and spirit, for the Christian believer, is released into the presence of God, set free from the confines of this mortal body. Absent from the body and present with the Lord (2 Corinthians 5:6), we will be more alive than ever! The Apostle Paul said:

> For to me, to live is Christ, and to die is gain. (Philippians 1:21)

The Psalmist said, "Precious in the sight of the Lord is the death of His saints" (Psalms 116:15). On the Mount of Transfiguration, Moses and Elijah appeared, talking to Jesus (Matthew 17:3), and to the dying thief, who called on Jesus, Jesus said:

> Assuredly, I say to you, today you will be with Me in Paradise. (Luke 23:43)

To these Biblical accounts (and there are more), we could add the experiences of those who have had after-death experiences before being resuscitated. Sticking to the Bible, for the believer, death is just a dark doorway that leads into the glorious presence of God. Resting in, and enjoying His presence, we await the day of resurrection, when we shall receive our incorruptible, immortal, resurrection body—to live in forever.

On that day, if we are alive at that moment, then our bodies shall be changed in an instant, into resurrection bodies. When Paul went to Thessalonica, he preached with great passion about the second coming of our Lord Jesus. When some of the Thessalonian believers passed away, there was some concern about what would happen to them. Paul writes:

> But I do not want you to be ignorant, brethren, concerning those who have fallen asleep (died), lest you sorrow as others who have no hope. For if we believe that Jesus died and rose again, even so God will bring with Him those who sleep (are resting) in Jesus. For this we say to you by the word of the Lord, that we who are alive and remain until the coming of

the Lord will by no means precede those who are asleep.

For the Lord Himself will descend from heaven with a shout, with the voice of the archangel and with the trumpet of God. And the dead in Christ will rise first. Then we who are alive and remain shall be caught up together with them in the clouds to meet the Lord in the air. And thus we shall always be with the Lord. Therefore comfort one another with these words. (1 Thessalonians 4:13-18)

Wonderful words of comfort—rest, resurrection, rapture, and reunion. The four 'Rs' of hope! Our final destination, the new heaven, and the new earth, where God will wipe away every tear and there shall be no more death, nor sorrow, no crying, and no more pain (Revelation 21:4). No doctors, no hospitals, and no undertakers!